IMMIGRANTS
in
HOBOKEN

IMMIGRANTS
_in_
HOBOKEN

One-Way Ticket, 1845–1985

CHRISTINA A. ZIEGLER-MCPHERSON

THE
History
PRESS

Published by The History Press
Charleston, SC   29403
www.historypress.net

Manufactured in the United States

ISBN 978.1.60949.163.5

Library of Congress Cataloging-in-Publication Data

Ziegler-McPherson, Christina A.
Immigrants in Hoboken : one way ticket, 1845-1985 / Christina A. Ziegler-McPherson.
p. cm.
Includes bibliographical references.
ISBN 978-1-60949-163-5
1. Hoboken (N.J.)--Emigration and immigration--History. 2. Immigrants--New Jersey--
Hoboken--History. 3. Hoboken (N.J.)--History. I. Title.
F144.H6Z54 2011
304.8'74926--dc22
2011011138

Contents

Acknowledgements

Thank you to Robert Foster, David Webster, Holly Metz and Sherrard Bostwick at the Hoboken Historical Museum; the staff of the Hoboken Public Library; the staff of the New Jersey Room of the Jersey City Main Library, especially librarians John Beekman and Cynthia Harris; Teofilio "Tom" Olivieri; Socorro Rivera; Delia Crespo; Ivonne Ballester; Elizabeth and Jerry Forman; George and Carmen Guzman; Angel and Gloria Padilla; Ines Garcia Keim; Raul Morales; Father Mike Guglielmolli of St. Francis Roman Catholic Church, Hoboken; Sister Norberta Hunnewinkel of the Hoboken Shelter; director of the Center for Puerto Rican Studies (Centro), Hunter College–CUNY, Dr. Edwin Meléndez; Centro associate director, chief librarian and archivist Dr. Alberto Hernandez Banuchi; and Centro senior archivist Pedro Juan Hernandez; William Miller; Father Alex Santorum and Ronnie Rosso at Our Lady of Grace Roman Catholic Church; Father Tom Crangle and Nancy Jefferson at St. Ann's Roman Catholic Church; Jessica Perez at St. Joseph's Roman Catholic Church; and Father Frank del Prate at Sts. Peter & Paul Roman Catholic Church.

Also, very big thanks to Scott McPherson, who drew tables and maps and was, once again, an excellent copyeditor.

Explanation of Terminology

Various terms—legal and theoretical—are used in this book, and therefore an explanation of the meaning of these terms is provided.

The term *German* is defined as immigrants from and citizens of the German states that now compose the Federal Republic of Germany, as well as German speakers from Austria, Switzerland, the Czech Republic and Alsace-Lorraine, which is now part of France, who identified with and participated in German community institutions in Hoboken. German speakers from Austria and Switzerland who identified themselves as Austrian or Swiss are noted as such. The term *German* implies no religion, unlike *Italian* and *Irish*, which assume Roman Catholicism. Irish Protestants are identified as such.

German American, *Irish American*, *Italian American*, etc., mean both a person of foreign birth who has naturalized and is thus an American citizen and the American-born children of immigrants.

Immigrant is defined as someone who has left his or her home country and is living in the United States. The more legalistic term *alien* refers to a non-U.S. citizen, who may or may not be an immigrant, such as a sailor who is in the country temporarily and does not intend to stay. The modern term *lawful permanent resident* is not used because this has a specific legal meaning under current U.S. immigration law and is therefore anachronistic. The children of immigrants who were born in the United States are both recognized as American citizens and considered members of their parents' immigrant community.

Native born refers to those persons born in the United States who did not participate in the immigrant experience and were not members of an immigrant community. This term is preferred over *American citizen*, since aliens can and did naturalize and become U.S. citizens.

PORT OF ENTRY
TO A CONTINENT

If Hoboken is a name known in the farthest corners of the rest of the world, if the children of Poland have heard of it and the old men of Jugoslavia [sic] attempt to write it, that fame is directly due to the fact that Hoboken is not merely a city, but the port of entry to a continent.[1]

The historian Oscar Handlin once said that the story of the United States is the story of immigration, and the same could be said for Hoboken, New Jersey. Hoboken's proximity to New York City has caused the mile-square city on the Hudson River to play an important, if oft overlooked, role in the processes of immigration to the United States in the nineteenth and twentieth centuries. When New York became the destination of choice for European immigrants in the 1840s, Hoboken became a key player in facilitating that immigration, becoming an immigrant community itself in the process. Immigrants were passengers for Hoboken's growing transportation industries, built the city's infrastructure and established prosperous businesses and community institutions.

Between 1845 and 1985, Hoboken played an important role in American migration history in three ways: 1) by facilitating immigration through the Port of New York to the interior United States with its extensive port and

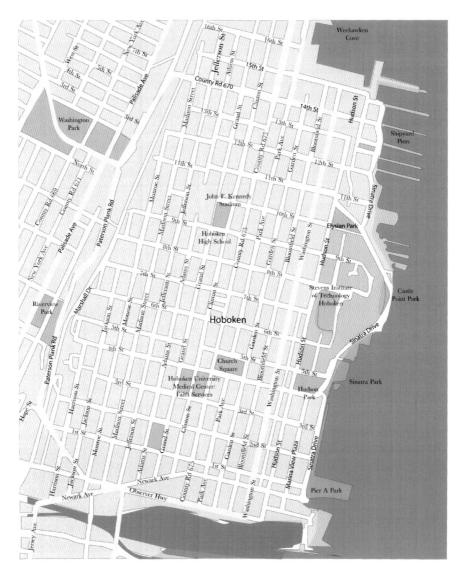

Hoboken, New Jersey, in 2010.

railroad facilities; 2) by becoming a destination itself as the American base for four major European shipping lines; and 3) by being an immigrant community for most of the city's 155-year-old history. A near-steady stream of immigration through and to Hoboken gave life in the city a dynamic quality. The years of immigration restriction and population decline between the world wars were an aberration in Hoboken's history, not the norm in its community life. Since the 1970s, Hoboken has been undergoing yet another demographic transformation: middle- and upper-class families and young professionals have turned the city into a bedroom community of New York City, thus proving that social change caused by the movement of people defines Hoboken as a city.

Hoboken's location on the New Jersey side of the Hudson River, one mile opposite Greenwich Village and midtown Manhattan, has meant that immigration to Hoboken has been closely tied to the city of New York for as long as immigrants have been coming to New York. Although Hoboken is legally in the state of New Jersey, the city's waterfront falls within the jurisdiction of the Port of New York and New Jersey, which also includes port facilities in Jersey City, Newark and Bayonne. The development of Hoboken into a major port facility in the mid- to late nineteenth century was a crucial part of the expansion of the Port of New York in response to increased trade with, and emigration from, Europe.

The United States, and New York City in particular, began to experience a steady increase in immigration in the early nineteenth century after the end of the Napoleonic Wars in 1815 made transatlantic travel safer and more profitable. Following clipper ship routes established in the 1820s, Europeans seeking greater economic opportunity and personal freedom began to immigrate to the United States, and increasingly these emigrants, as they were then called, sailed into New York Harbor.

The British Black Ball Line pioneered scheduled transatlantic sailing between Liverpool and New York beginning in 1818. Unlike other shipping companies, Black Ball's sailing ships left port on a fixed schedule, regardless of whether they had full cargoes. The popularity of more predictable sailing times resulted in immediate competition, and by 1825, there were at least three companies sailing nearly thirty so-called packet ships from Liverpool to New York.

Although these shipping companies made more money transporting high-paying cabin passengers and luxury freight goods than steerage passengers, the packet lines indirectly stimulated emigrant traffic on non-packet ships by siphoning away higher-value freight from the non-packets. Non-packet ships began carrying large numbers of steerage passengers to fill their increasingly empty cargo holds. For people traveling on packet ships, the regular sailing times allowed emigrants to save money that otherwise would have been spent on food and lodging while waiting for a ship to depart. This reduction in overall travel cost spurred many more Europeans to emigrate in the 1820s and 1830s.[2]

British sailing-packet lines dominated the transatlantic trade in the antebellum period, and so many of these early emigrants sailed from an English port, usually Liverpool, regardless of where their journeys originally began. In the 1850s, LeHavre, Bremen and Hamburg became major European ports catering to emigrant traffic.[3]

The cost of the passage varied, depending on the destination, but the price of a ticket to America dropped from about seven English pounds to between three and five English pounds (about twenty dollars) in the 1830s. And increasingly, many of these European passengers traveled with prepaid tickets sent to them by relatives already in America.[4]

It took approximately five or six weeks to cross the Atlantic (with good weather), and until 1855, steerage passengers were required to provide their own food, cooking utensils and even bedding.[5]

The packets carried their "farmyards" with a cow for milk and with sheep, pigs, and poultry; but those were for the cabin passengers, who were fed bountifully and served by obsequious Negro stewards. None of that was for the poor devils 'tween decks. Their passage money entitled them only to bread, salt meat, and a few other supplies. They not only had to bring most of their own food, but cook everything themselves. Grates were arranged on deck, but only a few might crowd around them at a time and the less aggressive might have to wait hours to get near a fire. In stormy weather, the grates were too exposed to be used at all and, as no fires were allowed below decks, it was a case of eating uncooked food or going hungry.[6]

Besides poor and inadequate food, antebellum emigrants endured cramped quarters with little to no privacy for sleeping, bathing or using the toilet. The air in the hold grew increasingly fetid with each passing day, and bad weather meant that passengers had to stay below deck for days at a time. Typhus, smallpox and cholera sometimes turned sailing ships into coffin ships, and there was always the threat of fire and shipwreck. In 1860, the rape and seduction of female passengers by crewmen or fellow passengers became such a problem that Congress passed an act "for the better protection of female passengers," requiring the seducer to either marry the woman or face imprisonment of not more than a year or a fine of not more than $1,000.[7] Lengthy and dangerous travel, bad weather, inadequate food, disease, sexual harassment—crossing the Atlantic was full of perils.

Government regulation of immigration to address these problems was negligible in this period, on both sides of the Atlantic. The first U.S. federal law regarding immigration was passed in 1819 and simply required a ship's captain to provide federal customs authorities a list of all passengers, detailing their names, sex, ages, occupations and countries of citizenship upon the ship's arrival at an American port. These ship manifests were kept on file with the Customs Office, which managed the ports.[8]

The State of New York's regulation of immigration was limited to an 1824 law that required each ship's master to post a bond of $300 per passenger to ensure that new arrivals would not become burdens on New York City charity (this was in response to the problem of ship captains abandoning sick passengers at Perth Amboy, New Jersey, to avoid New York's quarantine law).[9] Most American cities, including New York, required immigrants to report their arrival to the mayor's office soon after disembarking, and in the 1820s and 1830s, the number of newcomers was small enough to implement this policy without much difficulty.[10] Between 1820 and 1845, 1,181,285 immigrants entered the United States, an average of 47,251 persons per year, with many coming to New York.

TABLE 1. IMMIGRATION TO THE UNITED STATES, BY COUNTRY, 1820–1929

REGION AND COUNTRY OF LAST RESIDENCE[11]	1820–1829	1830–1839	1840–1849	1850–1859	1860–1869	1870–1879	1880–1889	1890–1899	1900–1909	1910–1919	1920–1929
All Countries	128,502	538,381	1,427,337	2,814,554	2,081,261	2,742,137	5,248,568	3,694,294	8,202,388	6,347,380	4,295,510
Europe	99,272	422,771	1,369,259	2,619,680	1,877,726	2,251,878	4,638,677	3,576,411	7,572,569	4,985,411	2,560,340
Austria-Hungary[12, 13]					3,375	60,127	314,787	534,059	2,001,376	1,154,727	60,891
Belgium	28	20	3,996	5,765	5,785	6,991	18,738	19,642	37,429	32,574	21,511
Bulgaria[14]								52	34,651	27,180	2,824
Czechoslovakia[15]											101,182
Denmark	173	927	671	3,227	13,553	29,278	85,342	56,671	61,227	45,830	34,406
Finland[16]											16,922
France	7,694	39,330	75,300	81,778	35,938	71,901	48,193	35,616	67,735	60,335	54,842
Germany[17]	5,753	124,726	385,434	976,072	723,734	751,769	1,445,181	579,072	328,722	174,227	386,634
Greece	17	49	17	32	51	209	1,807	12,732	145,402	198,108	60,774
Ireland[18]	51,617	170,672	656,145	1,029,486	427,419	422,264	674,061	405,710	344,940	166,445	202,854
Italy	430	225	1,476	8,643	9,853	46,296	267,660	603,761	1,930,475	1,229,916	528,133
Netherlands	1,105	1,377	7,624	11,122	8,387	1,4267	52,715	29,349	42,463	46,065	29,397
Norway-Sweden[19]	91	1,149	12,389	22,202	82,937	178,823	586,441	334,058	426,981	192,445	170,329
Poland[20]	19	366	105	1,087	1,886	11,016	42,910	107,793			223,316
Portugal[21]	177	820	196	1,299	2,083	13,971	15,186	25,874	65,154	82,489	44,829
Romania							5,842	6,808	57,322	13,566	67,810
Russia[22, 23]	86	280	520	423	1,670	35,177	182,698	450,101	1,501,301	1,106,998	61,604

Region and Country of Last Residence	1820–1829	1830–1839	1840–1849	1850–1859	1860–1869	1870–1879	1880–1889	1890–1899	1900–1909	1910–1919	1920–1929
Spain[24]	2,595	2,010	1,916	8,795	6,966	5,540	3,995	9,189	24,818	53,262	47,109
Switzerland	3,148	4,430	4,819	24,423	21,124	25,212	81,151	37,020	32,541	22,839	31,772
United Kingdom[25,26]	26,336	74,350	218,572	445,322	532,956	578,447	810,900	328,759	469,518	371,878	341,552
Yugoslavia[27]											49,215
Other Europe	3	40	79	4	9	590	1,070	145	514	6,527	22,434
Asia	34	55	121	36,080	54,408	134,128	71,151	61,285	299,836	269,736	126,740
China	3	8	32	35,933	54,028	133,139	65,797	15,268	19,884	20,916	30,648
India	9	38	33	42	50	166	247	102	3,026	3,478	2,076
Iran											208
Japan					138	193	1,583	13,998	139,712	77,125	42,057
Syria											5,307
Turkey	19	8	45	94	129	382	2,478	27,510	127,999	160,717	40,450
Other Asia		1	11	11	63	248	1,046	4,407	9,215	7,500	5,994
America	9,655	31,905	50,516	84,145	130,292	345,010	524,826	37,350	277,809	1,070,539	1,591,278
Canada, Newfoundland[28]	2,297	11,875	34,285	64,171	117,978	324,310	492,865	3,098	123,067	708,715	949,286
Mexico[29]	3,835	7,187	3,069	3,446	1,957	5,133	2,405	734	31,188	185,334	498,945
Caribbean[30]	3,061	11,792	11,803	12,447	8,751	14,285	27,323	31,480	100,960	120,860	83,482
Central America	57	94	297	512	70	173	279	649	7,341	15,692	16,511
South America	405	957	1,062	3,569	1,536	1,109	1,954	1,389	15,253	39,938	43,025

Region and Country of Last Residence[31]	1820–1829	1830–1839	1840–1849	1850–1859	1860–1869	1870–1879	1880–1889	1890–1899	1900–1909	1910–1919	1920–1929
Other America[31]											29
Africa	15	50	61	84	407	371	763	432	6,326	8,867	6,362
Egypt					4	29	145	51			1,063
Liberia	1	8	5	7	43	52	21	9			
South Africa					35	48	23	9			
Other Africa	14	42	56	77	325	242	574	363	6,326	8,867	5,299
Oceania	3	7	14	166	187	9,996	12,361	4,704	12,355	12,339	9,860
Australia	2	1	2	15		8,930	7,250	3,098	11,191	11,280	8,404
New Zealand						39	21	12			935
Other Oceania	1	6	12	151	187	1,027	5,090	1,594	1,164	1,059	521
Not specified[32]	19,523	83,593	7,366	74,399	18,241	754	790	14,112	33,493	488	930

Note: From 1820 to 1867, figures represent alien passenger arrivals at seaports; from 1868 to 1891 and 1895 to 1897, immigrant alien arrivals; from 1892 to 1894 and 1898 to 2007, immigrant aliens admitted for permanent residence; from 1892 to 1903, aliens entering by cabin class were not counted as immigrants.

Land arrivals were not completely enumerated until 1908. For this table, fiscal year 1843 covers 9 months ending September 1843; fiscal years 1832 and 1850 cover 15 months ending December 31 of the respective years; and fiscal year 1868 covers 6 months ending June 30, 1868.

Then, suddenly, the numbers jumped as political turmoil and economic collapse uprooted millions of Europeans in the mid-1840s. It began with famine. In 1845, a fungus struck Ireland's potato crop and then traveled east, destroying peasants' crops in Ireland and Western and Central Europe every year for the next three years. The ensuing famines caused hundreds of thousands of people to leave their rural homes and move first to European and English cities and then to the United States and Canada in search of work, land and other new opportunities.

In addition to the hundreds of thousands of Irish peasants, this migrant stream was populated by many Germans and Central Europeans, "small proprietors forced off the land by agricultural depression, spinners and handloom weavers unable to compete with English textiles flooding down the Rhine, skilled shoemakers and furniture makers facing proletarianization, and handfuls of merchants and manufacturers frustrated by economic stagnation and political repression."[33] The failure of the democratic revolutions of 1848–49 in France, Germany and Austria-Hungary caused many skilled craftsmen, small shopkeepers, bourgeois professionals and liberal and radical intellectuals to emigrate. In 1850 alone, nearly 370,000 immigrants entered the United States, most from Ireland, Germany and Great Britain.

But as immigration increased, so did the fears of native New Yorkers. Several scandals involving mistreatment of immigrants aboard ship, fears of pauperism and disease being imported into the city (New York suffered a yellow fever epidemic in 1822 and then cholera in 1832 and 1849) and ship captains' continued efforts to avoid the city's quarantine rules prompted New Yorkers to pursue new kinds of regulation.

The most significant pressure for a new policy came from the city's new immigrant mutual aid societies, which had been providing food, medical care, burial services, charitable relief, employment and housing services and other assistance to their destitute countrymen since the beginning of the famine exodus. Increasingly overwhelmed by the ever-growing number of sick and starving Irish and Germans being deposited on the piers of New York, the members of the German Society and the Irish Emigrant Society successfully pressured the New York state legislature to create the New York State Board of Commissioners of Emigration in 1847 to regulate conditions at the port. The new board was composed of the mayors of New York City and Brooklyn (still a separate city until 1898), representatives of the German Society and the Irish Emigrant Society and six gubernatorial appointees. Six of the original ten members were members of the Irish association the Friendly Sons of St. Patrick, reflecting the growing influence of Irish immigrants in New York City politics. German Society leader Gulian C. Verplanck was president of the board for several years and oversaw the initiation and development of the commission's programs. The legislature also revoked the $300 bond law and replaced it with a head tax of $1.50 per passenger and a hospital tax to pay for medical care for sick immigrants.[34]

> With these funds, the commissioners assumed responsibility for both the poor relief and the hospitals. The marine hospital at Staten Island was reserved for contagious cases. For the non-contagious hospitalization and dispensary treatment, to which each immigrant was entitled for a year, as well as for a place of refuge for the infirm and indigent, a large establishment was set up on Ward's Island at Hell Gate. From 1847 to 1860, the commissioners spent more than five million in caring for 893,000 immigrants, just a third of those who arrived at the port during those years.[35]

But these new state regulations met fierce resistance from shipowners, who challenged the commission's right to collect the head tax all the way to the U.S. Supreme Court—and won in 1849. Undaunted, the commissioners successfully lobbied the legislature to grant them $60,000 to pay for their charitable work and to revise the law to allow the commission to manage the Marine Hospital and to collect the head tax, which was raised to $2 in 1853.[36]

Besides providing free medical care, temporary charitable relief, temporary housing and burial services for destitute, sick and dying immigrants, the commission also licensed boardinghouses, "runners" (recruiters for hotels) and "forwarders," a type of guide who helped immigrants transfer to trains and ferries. Boardinghouse keepers were required to provide information about their rates in English, French, German, Dutch and Welsh, while runners had to identify themselves with a special "licensed emigrant runner" tag on their hats or vests.[37]

By the 1850s, the Manhattan piers were crowded with runners, teamsters, luggage porters, money changers, food vendors, pickpockets and other thieves awaiting the daily ship arrivals and their human cargo. To better manage this chaotic situation, the emigration commissioners received permission from the legislature to establish a single landing place where immigrants could collect their luggage, bathe and change clothes, exchange money, buy train tickets and food and get information about travel routes west or jobs and housing in New York. On August 1, 1855, the commission opened its new Emigrant Depot at the former concert hall, Castle Garden, in Battery Park.[38] This facility was to be the nation's main immigration station for the next thirty-five years.

In his memoirs, Columbia University physicist Dr. Michael Pupin described his interview at Castle Garden in the fall of 1874 upon arriving from his native Serbia:

> *Presently the ship passed by Castle Garden, and I heard some one say: "There is the Gate to America." An hour or so later we all stood at the gate. The immigrant ship,* Westphalia, *landed at Hoboken and a tug took us to Castle Garden. We were carefully examined and cross-examined, and when my turn came the examining officials shook their heads and seemed to find me wanting. I confessed that I had only five cents in my pocket and had no relatives here, and that I knew of nobody in this country except Franklin, Lincoln, and Harriet Beecher Stowe, whose "Uncle Tom's Cabin" I had read in a translation. One of the officials, who had one leg only, and walked with a crutch, seemed much impressed by this remark, and looking very kindly into my eyes and with a merry twinkle in his eye he said in German: "You showed good taste when you picked your American acquaintances." I learned later that he was a Swiss who had served in the Union army during the Civil War. I confessed also to the examining officials that I had no training in the arts and crafts, but that I was anxious to learn, and that this desire had brought me to America… The Swiss veteran who walked on crutches, having lost one of his legs in the Civil War, was particularly attentive while I was being cross-examined, and nodded approvingly whenever I scored a point with my answers. He whispered something to the other officials, and they finally informed me that I could pass on, and I was conducted promptly to the Labor Bureau of Castle Garden. My Swiss friend looked me up a little later and informed me that the examiners had made an exception in my favor and admitted me, and that I must look sharp and find a job as soon as possible.[39]*

Arrival at Castle Garden, a wood engraving originally published in *Frank Leslie's Illustrated Newspaper* on January 20, 1866 (vol. 21, p. 280). *Library of Congress.*

Registering Emigrants at Castle Garden, a wood engraving originally published in *Frank Leslie's Illustrated Newspaper* on January 20, 1866 (vol. 21, pp. 280–81). *Library of Congress.*

Port of Entry to a Continent

Passing the Inspecting Physician, a wood engraving originally published in *Frank Leslie's Illustrated Newspaper* on January 20, 1866 (vol. 21, p. 281). *Library of Congress.*

The Labor Exchange—Emigrants on the Battery in Front of Castle Garden. A wood engraving by Stanley Fox, originally published in *Harper's Weekly* on August 15, 1868. *Library of Congress.*

Pupin was lucky. The state examiners were primarily concerned with keeping out paupers and others who lacked an obvious means of financial support, a power to exclude that had been upheld by the Supreme Court in 1847 in *City of New York v. Milne*. In the Milne case, the court had agreed with New York that states had the right to exercise police power within their boundaries, and this included excluding undesirable persons. Immigration restriction by states in the mid-nineteenth century was thus likened to a form of quarantine.[40]

The transformation of Castle Garden into the Emigrant Depot created controversy in New York, particularly among the residents of the city's First Ward, who objected to the construction of a public facility for "paupers" in their neighborhood.[41]

The loudest protesters, however, were the men who worked the piers, assisting immigrants in transferring themselves and their luggage to western-bound trains and/or hotels; changing money; selling food and beverages; and recruiting for jobs at the docks. On August 3, 1855, the first day Castle Garden received a shipload of passengers, runners, angry at the new tall fence that kept them out of the facility, threw rocks at commission president and German Society representative Rudolph Garrigue and other commission employees. The violence prompted Irish commissioner John A. Kennedy to brandish a revolver in defense.

Runners and residents of the First Ward organized two mass "indignation meetings," the first attended by three thousand people and the second by several hundred, in the first week of August to protest what they alleged was the corruption of the emigration commissioners and their conspiracy to profit off immigrants themselves. Articulating the rhetoric and values of Jacksonian America, the runners argued that competition was a core value of American society and that the Emigration Depot represented a monopoly (as well as a loss of business to themselves). Other arguments against the depot were that a public space should not be privatized (although the Emigration Commission was a joint state-municipal entity) and that immigrants should be received first on an island in the harbor, not in the city, for public health reasons.

Although most of the people demonstrating against the new Emigrant Depot were working-class Americans, there were also many German and Irish immigrants who disliked the upper-class commissioners and, in particular, the leaders of the German Society and Irish Emigrant Society.

Nor were the hostile audiences at the "indignation meetings" exclusively working class; such prominent New Yorkers as Cornelius Vanderbilt, Stephen Whitney and Jacob Roosevelt agreed to serve on a committee opposed to Castle Garden's new function.[42]

But despite the protests, the Emigrant Depot at Castle Garden was to be in business until 1892, when the federal government took over the regulation and business of immigration and opened Ellis Island.

The opening of Castle Garden was part of a larger effort in the United States to improve the migration experience. For immigrants arriving in New York in the antebellum period, crime and fraud upon their arrival in America constituted only one more problem in a long series of hardships that had begun weeks, even months, before.

Only through the imposition of regulations by both the U.S. and European states did travel conditions for transatlantic passengers improve. In laws passed in 1847 and 1855, the U.S. federal government sought to prevent the overcrowding of ships through minimum space requirements and the requirement that the travelers be fed at least one hot meal per day. In

Immigrants on the Steerage Deck of the Steamship Germanic. A wood engraving originally published in *Frank Leslie's Illustrated Newspaper* on July 2, 1887 (pp. 324–25). *Library of Congress.*

"*Hoboken in New Jersey, the Seat of Mr. John Stevens*, drawn, engraved & published by W. Birch, Springland near Bristol, Pennsylv'a," 1808. *Library of Congress.*

1882, the United States imposed a head tax and prohibited the admission of Chinese immigrants, people liable to become public charges, the physically and mentally disabled and convicts. In 1887, U.S. immigration law was amended to require that inadmissible immigrants be returned to their ports of departure at the expense of the company that had transported them.[43] These measures, as well as similar laws passed by German states and Great Britain, forced the shipping companies to improve conditions on board ships and to develop large port facilities in Europe where they screened would-be immigrants to America for disease, disability and criminality.

Gradually, transatlantic travel became faster, safer and more comfortable. And with the opening of Castle Garden and the work of the New York Board of Emigration Commissioners, immigrants were assured of some degree of assistance and protection upon their arrival in America.

When New York City began experiencing its first large surge in immigration in the 1840s, Hoboken was a small village known primarily for being the home of the Elysian Fields, a wooded picnic pleasure ground

Sybil's Cave and Riverwalk, circa 1880. *Hoboken Historical Museum.*

located between what are now Tenth and Fifteenth Streets and west from the Hudson River to Clinton Street. The Elysian Fields and its River Walk promenade were developed by Colonel John Stevens, who bought the land that now encompasses the city of Hoboken from the State of New Jersey in 1784 for 18,360 British pounds (about $90,000).[44] The State of New Jersey had confiscated the property from William Bayard after he sided with the British during the American Revolution. (Stevens's son, Edwin A. Stevens, married Martha Bayard, thus reconnecting the Bayard family to its old estate). John Stevens built a stately Georgian-style mansion on Castle Point overlooking the Hudson and gridded out the rest of his New Jersey property. He sold lots in the eastern portion at an auction held at the Tontine Coffeehouse in New York City in 1804 and sold a large tract in the marshy western part of town to Samuel and Robert Swartwout in 1814 to develop as farmland.[45] Stevens also pioneered ferry service on the Hudson River, bringing thousands of New Yorkers across the river on steam-powered ferryboats to recreate on his property from the 1820s to the 1850s.[46]

Despite these promotional efforts, Hoboken remained small and largely undeveloped for the first half of the nineteenth century. "By 1829 there was a post office, four hotels, four groceries, three smithies, one wheelwright, two carpenter shops, one livery stable, one distillery, one steel manufactory, three schools, and a population of between four

and five hundred persons."[47] In 1834, a visitor to the Elysian Fields was less prosaic, describing Hoboken as "built chiefly on one street, it contains about one hundred dwellings, three licensed taverns (and many unlicensed ones), four or five stores, and between six and seven hundred inhabitants."[48] Or, as a Catholic temperance advocate lamented in 1843, only seventy-one houses but fifty-nine "rum-shops."[49]

This was soon to change, and immigration was the driving force behind that change. When immigrants began crowding into New York City in the 1840s and 1850s, Hoboken did not have piers or rail terminals to transport settlers west. Unlike on the Manhattan side of the Hudson, the New Jersey side of the shoreline, especially around Hoboken and Jersey City, was mostly marsh, except for a few hills, including the one-hundred-foot-high Castle Point. In addition, in the aftermath of the American Revolution, New York State had claimed that its state boundary went as far as the high-tide water line on the New Jersey side of the Hudson, thus thwarting economic development on the Jersey side of the river for several years. It was not until 1834—when the two states agreed to a compact ratified by Congress to set the state boundary between them as the midpoint of the Hudson—that economic development of the Hudson County shoreline was legally feasible.[50] It would take another several decades of determined engineering to fill in and stabilize the marshy shoreline.

A Baseball Match at the Elysian Fields.
A wood engraving originally
published in *Harper's Weekly* on
October 15, 1889 (vol. 3, no. 146,
pp. 664–65). *Library of Congress.*

But one thing Hoboken did have in the first part of the nineteenth century
was convenient ferry service to and from Manhattan. Colonel Stevens had
run ferries between his Hudson County estate and lower Manhattan as early
as 1804, but regular ferry service on the steamboat *Hoboken* began in 1822
and went between Hoboken and Barclay Street. The Hoboken Steamboat
Ferry Company, which was owned (like most things in Hoboken) by the
Stevens family, inaugurated a second line from Hoboken to Christopher
Street in Greenwich Village in 1838, the same year John Stevens died
and his heirs organized the Hoboken Land & Improvement Company to
develop and manage the family's real estate holdings.[51] With its strategic
location on the Jersey side of the Hudson and easy access to Manhattan, the
Land & Improvement Company was able to attract transatlantic shipping
companies and railroads to Hoboken just when immigration to New York
was beginning to increase.

The shippers were the first to arrive. In the 1840s and 1850s, the vast
majority of the ships arriving at the Port of New York were owned by British
companies and came from Liverpool. But in the 1860s, European shipping
lines sailing from Bremen, Hamburg, Le Havre, Antwerp and Rotterdam
began competing aggressively with the British for the emigrant trade.

Looking for more space than was available around Manhattan, the
Hamburg-America Packet Company, which was organized in 1847, built
a pier at the foot of First and Newark Streets in 1863 to provide service

New York from Bergen Hill, Hoboken. An engraving by Robert Loudan, originally published as an extra supplement to the Illustrated London News on August 19, 1876. *Library of Congress.*

from Hamburg to Hoboken. North German Lloyd Steamship Company, which began providing passenger transport from Bremen to New York in 1857, constructed a pier at Third Street in 1864. The Scandinavia Line (initially called Thingvalla) built its pier at Fourth Street in 1879 and sailed between Hoboken and Copenhagen, Stettin and Christiania, while Holland America moved its pier from Jersey City to Hoboken's Fifth Street in 1891.[52]

By 1892, when the federal government opened its immigration station at Ellis Island, Hoboken's waterfront was crowded with large steamships carrying thousands of passengers. Nearly every day, a ship arrived. In the 1890s, Hamburg-America had twenty-six ships that sailed to and from Hoboken three times a week; North German Lloyd had fourteen vessels. Holland America had only nine ships at the turn of the century but provided weekly service to Hoboken, as did Scandinavia America, with four ships.[53]

Once the European steamship companies began sailing regularly to and from Hoboken, New York rail companies became interested in the once-sleepy resort community. In the 1840s, 1850s and 1860s, railroad companies had been busy with the Herculean task of filling in the Jersey City marshlands from Harsimus Cove to Communipaw to allow for rail

New York and Brooklyn, with Jersey City and Hoboken Water Front. A chromolithograph by Charles R. Parsons and Lyman Atwater, originally published by Currier and Ives, 1877. *Library of Congress.*

development.[54] By the end of the nineteenth century, five major railroad depots had been built along the New Jersey side of the Hudson, with each providing ferryboat service for passengers to cross to and from Manhattan. Although each station was owned by a separate company, the railroads shared track and terminal space at various times. Weekhawken was the eastern terminus of the New York Central Railroad, while Jersey City had three terminals: the Erie in the north, the Pennsylvania Railroad depot at Paulus Hook and the Central Railroad of New Jersey in the southern part of town. Hoboken was the eastern terminus of the Delaware, Lackawanna & Western Railroad, which bought the Hoboken Ferry Company in 1903.[55] The Erie Railroad also had a branch terminal at the northern border of Hoboken, the West Shore Railroad had a depot at the southern end and the Hoboken Manufacturers' Railroad, also called the Shore Road, connected Hoboken with the rest of the New Jersey rail system.[56] This connection of railroad and ferry facilities to the steamship companies' piers allowed Hoboken to play a crucial role in the transportation of immigrants arriving at the Port of New York in the late nineteenth and early twentieth centuries.

This boom in transportation facilitated a corresponding boom in population in Hoboken. As immigration to the Port of New York surged in the 1850s and 1860s, immigrants to New York began to cross the Hudson and settle in Hoboken, as well as in nearby Jersey City and Weehawken. In 1840, Hoboken was not large enough to register in the Sixth U.S. Census, but Hudson County had 9,489 people, most of them native-born Americans of British or Dutch descent.[57] In 1850, the first year Hoboken was counted as a distinct community in the census, the town had 2,668 people. By 1860, Hoboken had 9,662 residents (an increase of more than 262 percent) and was large enough to have wards, reflecting its status as a newly incorporated city (in 1855). In 1870, the city's population had again more than doubled, to 20,297 people, and slightly more than half of its residents were foreign born (10,334 foreign born versus 9,963 native born).[58] By 1890, Hoboken had 43,638 residents, 17,364 (40 percent) of them foreign born, with many native-born residents the children of immigrants.[59]

Table 2. Population of Hoboken, 1850–1890

Year	Population	Increase (%)
1850	2,668	
1860	9,662	262
1870	20,297	110
1880	30,999	53
1890	43,648	41

(U.S. Census)

Table 3. Hoboken Population by Ward, Race, and Nationality, 1850–1860

Year	Total	Ward 1	Ward 2	Ward 3
1850	2,668			
Ethnicity:				
White	2,639			
Free colored	29			

Year	Total	Ward 1	Ward 2	Ward 3
1860	9,659			
Ethnicity:				
White	9,621	3,987	2,455	3,179
Free colored	38	13	25	0

(U.S. Census)

TABLE 4. HOBOKEN POPULATION BY WARD, RACE, AND NATIONALITY, 1870–1890

Year	Total	Ward 1	Ward 2	Ward 3	Ward 4
1870	20,297	4,987	3,610	6,853	4,847
Ethnicity:					
White	20,225	4,983	3,577	6,849	4,846
Colored	42	4	33	4	1
Origin:					
Native	9,963	2,447	1,852	3,608	2,056
Foreign	10,334	2,540	1,758	3,245	2,791
1880	30,999				
Ethnicity:					
White	30,915	N/A	N/A	N/A	N/A
Colored	74	N/A	N/A	N/A	N/A
Origin:					
Native	18,004	N/A	N/A	N/A	N/A
Foreign	12,995	N/A	N/A	N/A	N/A
1890	43,648	10,063	5,765	14,859	12,961

(U.S. Census)

Immigration to Hoboken was part of the mass movement of people to reach New York in the mid-nineteenth century. As in New York, virtually all Hoboken's immigrants came from Germany and Ireland, with a sizeable minority coming from England and Scotland. Of Hoboken's 2,668 residents in 1850, approximately half—1,030 people—were foreign born. Of those, 419 were Irish, 263 were German and nearly 260 were British, mostly

English. This is the demographic profile that would define Hoboken for the rest of the nineteenth century.[60]

The occupations of Hoboken's immigrant and native-born populations differed considerably according to nationality. More men in Hoboken worked as artisans and merchants than in any other occupation, although a large number worked in the shipping industry as well. Native-born Americans predominated in all of these sectors and, not surprisingly, made up the majority of the city's small professional class. In 1850, Americans were commonly employed as carpenters, masons, clerks, ship's carpenters, boatmen and engineers. In the luxury goods trades, Hoboken had eight American-born jewelers. Only in the clothing-related industries were there more Germans than Americans, and there were more Irish men working in the food industries (butcher, baker, etc.) and as unskilled laborers than there were native-born men in those industries.

Although the vast majority of Irish-born men were unskilled laborers, there were Irish artisans and professionals in Hoboken in 1850, reflecting the fact that many of Hoboken's Irish had migrated before the Great Famine of 1845–52. There were as many Irish as Germans working as skilled craftsmen, although English and Germans predominated in the luxury goods trades.

Most Germans were skilled craftsmen, but there were also sixteen German-born merchants and nine German clerks. Very few Germans worked as unskilled laborers. Germans predominated in the clothing industry, largely due to the seven German cane makers and four German tailors in Hoboken in 1850.

British-born immigrants were more like white Americans socioeconomically, clustered in the skilled and luxury goods trades and the professions. Hoboken had five Scottish merchants, three English merchants and four English and four Scottish-born clerks. In the skilled and luxury goods trades, there were six English carpenters and five jewelers, including one who specialized in watches. Four of the city's eight printers were English. Two of Hoboken's four clergymen were born in England, and interestingly, both the town's constable and justice of the peace were English. Hoboken's only architect was English.

The city's small Swiss population was composed mostly of merchants and clerks, although Hoboken also had two Swiss hotel keepers and two Swiss watch-case makers. The only miller and boot maker in town were both Swiss. Whether these Swiss were German speaking or French speaking is unknown because the census of 1850 did not ask about mother tongues. French immigrants in Hoboken worked mainly in the skilled trades as turners and in the luxury goods industries, making watches and maps. One of Hoboken's two physicians was French, and the city also had a French-born hotel keeper in 1850.

Although New York City's immigrant population diversified dramatically in the late nineteenth century, Hoboken's ethnic composition remained relatively homogeneous. Between the Civil War and World War I, Hoboken remained primarily a German town, with strong Celtic flavoring. The city's third immigrant group, people from Great Britain, blended easily into the city's native-born, Anglo-American population.

In 1890, Hoboken had 43,648 people, nearly 40 percent of whom were foreign born. Of its 17,364 foreign-born residents, nearly 80 percent were either German or Irish, with German speakers predominating. Among English-speaking immigrants, Hoboken had 3,862 Irish-born residents and nearly 1,500 residents born in the British Isles or English-speaking Canada. Immigrants from Italy and the Scandinavian countries formed small but distinct communities. Hoboken had more residents born at sea (5) than it did Bohemians (4). (Bohemia was then a part of the Austro-Hungarian empire and is now a region of the Czech Republic.) More French and Dutch lived in Hoboken than did Slavs. At a time when hundreds of thousands of Jews were fleeing czarist pogroms in Russia and transforming New York's *Kleindeutschland* (Little Germany) on the Lower East Side into an Eastern European Jewish neighborhood, Hoboken had only 54 Russians and 20 Poles.[61] Hoboken also had only 26 Chinese and 76 black residents, nearly all of them native born but several with African-born parents.

This demography was representative of New Jersey's overall immigration experience; Irish, German and English immigrants composed the vast majority of the state's foreign-born population in the nineteenth century, and it was not until the early twentieth century that Southern and Eastern Europeans came to predominate.[62] Yet Hoboken's German and Irish immigrants created very different communities, reflecting differences in reasons for emigration, socioeconomic background, religion and native culture.

2

LITTLE BREMEN

Germans have been immigrating to America in large numbers for more than three hundred years, and there have been German speakers living in the New York City area since the founding of New Amsterdam by the Dutch in 1624. The German immigration to America has always been very diverse, marked by differences in country of origin, regional cultures, religion, socioeconomic class, reasons for migration and even language (German dialects varied considerably from one another). Although nineteenth-century government documents often referred to immigration from "Germany," there was no German nation-state until 1871 (and that new state excluded a large number of German speakers). Instead, German-speaking immigrants came from the forty-one principalities and city-states of the former German Confederation (which included Austria and the German-speaking sections of the Czech Republic) and Switzerland.

In Hoboken, German-speaking immigrants built thriving businesses and important community institutions, but the diversity that defined German immigration meant that Hoboken's German community was also often divided, except when external threats to the German language and culture brought people together. Germans turned Hoboken into "Little Bremen," but they never controlled the city's politics in the same the way that they shaped Hoboken's cultural and economic institutions.

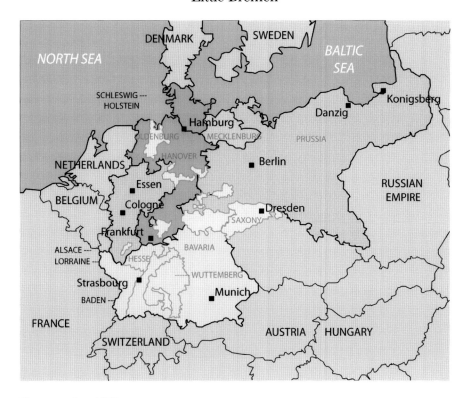

Germany, circa 1870.

Hoboken's German community was an extension of New York City's Little Germany, located initially on the Lower East Side of Manhattan. Heavy immigration from German-speaking states from the 1840s to the 1880s made New York City the third largest German city in the world after Berlin and Vienna, and German immigrants and their children composed one third of New York's population in 1875. Brooklyn also had a large, prosperous German community, and the villages of Queens were also heavily German in the mid- to late nineteenth century.[63]

New York's and Hoboken's German-speaking communities initially came from southern and western German states, such as Bavaria, Baden, Württemburg, Hesse and the Palatinate, through which the Rhine River flowed.[64] These Rhinelanders had a long tradition of migration within Europe and to America; the term *wanderlust* came from this region of Germany.[65] After the American Civil War, Germans in the New York City area tended to come from Eastern Germany, particularly Prussia, but states that had sent many migrants before 1870 continued to do so after, only in slightly fewer numbers.[66] Hoboken saw a surge of Prussian immigration in the 1860s; out of more than five thousand German-born residents living in Hoboken in 1870, thirty-nine hundred came from Prussia, whereas the census of 1860 had reported no Prussian immigration at all. The few Eastern Germans who immigrated to Hoboken in the 1850s came from Mecklenburg, Berlin and Pomerania. In the 1860s and 1870s, most Hoboken Germans came from Prussia, Hanover, Bavaria, Bremen, Baden and Württemberg.[67]

TABLE 5. HOBOKEN'S GERMAN POPULATION, 1880–1930

YEAR	TOTAL POPULATION	GERMAN BORN	NATIVE BORN TO GERMAN PARENTS	GERMANS AS % OF POPULATION
1880	30,999	6,261	5,064	37
1890	43,648	9,949	7,926	41
1900	59,364	10,843	10,056	35
1910	70,324	10,018	8,118	26
1920	68,166	5,917	N/A	N/A
1930	59,261	5,864	N/A	N/A

(U.S. Census)

TABLE 6. GERMAN AMERICANS AND THE GERMAN STATE OF ORIGIN OF PARENTS, 1880

GERMAN-SPEAKING STATE	NJ BORN(BOTH PARENTS)	NJ BORN(1 PARENT)	NY BORN(BOTH PARENTS)	NY BORN(1 PARENT)	OTHER U.S. BORN	TOTAL
North						**2,443**
Holstein	24	97	14	21	124	280
Schleswig	0	2	0	4	5	11
Hamburg	31	114	11	20	184	360
Brunswick	3	44	0	12	43	102

Little Bremen

German-speaking State	NJ born (both parents)	NJ born (1 parent)	NY born (both parents)	NY born (1 parent)	Other U.S. born	Total
Bremen	53	133	23	35	331	575
Hanover	196	250	85	73	511	1,115
Central						**1,278**
Westphalia	1	23	7	2	26	59
Hesse	18	85	14	44	82	243
Thuringia	0	0	3	0	9	12
Frankfurt	0	0	0	0	1	1
Saxony	55	123	20	53	200	451
Weimar	0	7	0	0	3	10
Oldenburg	38	56	17	11	132	254
Nassau	3	14		0	9	26
Darmstadt	10	113		2	70	195
Cassel (Kassel)	4	5		0	18	27
Southwest						**2,236**
Alsace	17	27	14	4	51	113
Baden	84	169	40	92	241	626
Württemberg	60	125	42	49	235	511
Stuttgart	0	0	0	0	0	0
Bavaria	110	291	65	121	399	986
East						**3,275**
Prussia	584	500	253	271	1,410	3,018
Pomerania	0	0	0	0	1	1
Mecklenburg	2	50	5	20	57	134
Brandenburg	0	2	0	0	1	3
Berlin	15	24	4	8	66	117
Breslau	0	1	0	0	1	2
Other Germany	75	39	47	32	2,345	2,538
Total	**1,383**	**2,294**	**664**	**874**	**6,555**	**11,770**

(U.S. Census, 1880)

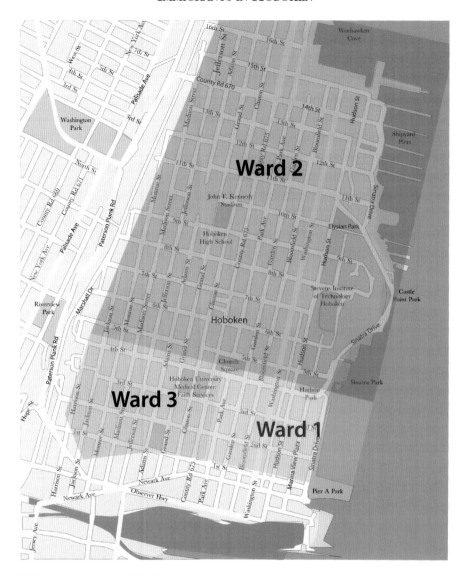

Hoboken wards, circa 1855–75.

Germans could be found living on almost every street in Hoboken, but certain areas had higher concentrations of Germans than others. In the 1850s, the city's First Ward, in the southeast part of town, had twice as many Germans as the Second and Third Wards, although the Third Ward in the western part of town had a large German population as well. The wealthy Second Ward around Castle Point and the former Stevens Estate on the

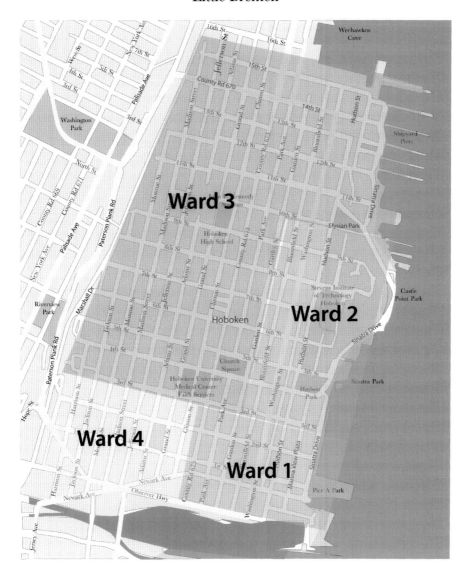

Hoboken wards, circa 1879–90.

Hudson River had the fewest immigrants of any Hoboken neighborhood. In the census of 1870, the First and Third Wards still had high concentrations of Germans. In the 1880s, the first two blocks of Washington had many German residents, with few Anglo-Americans or Irish. The first block of First Street was also highly German. By 1910, Germans were clustered heavily in the First Ward but could be found evenly distributed throughout the rest of the city.[68]

Germans in New York City tended to self-segregate according to ancestral homeland, and this clustering further encouraged endogamy (marrying within the ethnic group), which was very high for Germans in the nineteenth century, between 92.0 and 97.5 percent (depending on the decade).[69]

Hoboken was a smaller and slightly less diverse version of New York's *Kleindeutschland*, but Hoboken's small geographic size meant that Germans had less opportunity to self-segregate by ancestral state than in Manhattan or Brooklyn. Instead of being able to cluster in certain wards, German Hobokenites who wanted to live with or near people from their home states had to try to find housing on the same street or even in the same building, which was not always possible.

But in the 1860s, Germans in Hoboken began to develop their own neighborhoods based on their states of origin. In 1870, more Prussians, for example, lived in the First Ward than in any other area, whereas Bavarians preferred to live in the Fourth Ward, away from the heavily Prussian First Ward. Württembergers preferred the First Ward, while Badeners concentrated in the Second Ward, with many Badeners also living in the First and Fourth Wards. Saxons were evenly distributed among the First, Third and Fourth Wards in the 1860s and early 1870s.[70] When given the choice, Germans from Prussia and Mecklenburg were slightly more likely to live together and to live apart from southern Germans, particularly Bavarians. When such segregation was not possible, an apparently important criterion for Germans was not to live in proximity to Irish immigrants. Whether this prejudice was ethnic, linguistic or religious is not known.[71]

TABLE 7. GERMANS BY WARD AND GERMAN STATE OF ORIGIN, 1860

Region	Total	Ward 1	Ward 2	Ward 3
Germany	842	440	118	233
Bavaria	119	34	47	39
Baden	114	30	45	39
Bremen	100	44	34	22

(U.S. Census, 1860)

TABLE 8. GERMANS BY WARD AND GERMAN STATE OF ORIGIN, 1870

Region	Total	Ward 1	Ward 2	Ward 3	Ward 4
Saxony	106	31	7	32	34
Baden	282	71	85	57	72
Württemberg	261	86	56	48	74
Prussia	3,895	1,115	830	1,020	836
Bavaria	309	98	31	30	150
Brunswick	32	7	1	15	9
Hesse	34	0	6	28	0

(U.S. Census, 1870)

Although regional prejudices and preferences persisted in the late nineteenth century, German Hobokenites were more concerned about marrying someone of the same religion than someone from the same part of Germany. German immigrants lived in all parts of Hoboken, often in the same buildings or next door to people from different German states, and so were more likely to meet future marriage partners at church, where the crucial question of religious compatibility was already resolved. Only Hanoverians were more likely to marry persons also from Hanover than from another part of Germany.[72] Interfaith marriage was rare, although when it did occur, it tended to be between Protestants of different denominations but within the same ethnic group. Marriage between Catholics and Protestants was uncommon.[73]

Germans occupied nearly every strata of socioeconomic position in Hoboken, from successful business entrepreneurs to unskilled laborers, longshoremen, luggage porters and domestic servants. Many Germans were artisans and skilled craftsmen, clerks, small store owners and saloon or restaurant owners. In 1850, Hoboken boasted two German-born portrait painters, three other Germans who identified themselves to census enumerators as "artists" and two German painters of china. Hoboken's only daguerreotypist was German born, as was the city's only editor. But merchant, cabinetmaker, clerk, cane maker, carpenter, tailor and barkeeper were the most common occupations held by Germans in 1850. By the 1880s, Hoboken had a sizeable number of German cigar makers; several cigar makers lived at 148 Clinton Street, combining work and residence.

Some of the most prominent German American businessmen in Hoboken were William Keuffel and Hermann Esser, the founders of the instrument-manufacturing firm Keuffel & Esser (1866), whose factory was at the corner of Third and Adams Streets until it was converted into housing in 1975; and Edward Weissenborn, who founded American Lead Pencil Company in 1860. Leather goods makers Lehman and Laudnitz left New York in 1888 and built a large plant at Willow Avenue and Ferry Street (now Observer Highway) that operated into the late twentieth century.[74]

In the late 1840s and early 1850s, Hoboken received many prominent refugees from the failed revolutions of 1848, including the South German radical S.L. Kapff, who opened a saloon in Hoboken and was arrested in 1853 for violating the city's Sunday closing ordinance; the anarchist theorist and journalist Karl Heinzen, who gilded picture frames in an effort to support his family; and, briefly, Colonel Georg von Amsberg, who fought first in the Hungarian revolution of 1848–49 and then with the Forty-fifth New York Regiment during the American Civil War.[75] Other important "Forty-Eighters" who settled in Hoboken were Dr. A.W. Rittler of Altenburg and Dr. Hans Kudlich, a Silesian who had been a leader in the Vienna Parliament and had fought with the Vienna student legion before fleeing first to Switzerland and then to the United States. Both Rittler and Kudlich practiced medicine in Hoboken for many years.[76]

Despite the presence and influence of the Forty-Eighters, most Germans in Hoboken were more interested and active in politics in America than in Europe. But initially, they were not sure whether to join one of the main American political parties or attempt to organize themselves into an ethnic voting bloc. In 1854, the earliest election year in which the first German immigrants of 1848–49 were eligible to vote as new American citizens, a group of Germans met at Hofer's Hotel in Hoboken to discuss the idea of forming a German political party. Although Germans did not create an ethnic-based political party, the group did create the Hoboken German Union Club.[77] A few years later, in 1860, as the antislavery debate intensified, radical German clubs in Hoboken were organized to support army explorer John C. Frémont as the Republican candidate for president, but they eventually endorsed Abraham Lincoln.[78] Although many Germans from New York and New Jersey fought for the Union in the Civil War, none of the 177 men who served in a volunteer regiment from Hoboken had German names.

Besides the issue of slavery, the other major issue that motivated Germans to become involved in local politics was the question of alcohol control. By the 1850s, the temperance movement was strong, and virtually all communities restricted the sale and consumption of alcohol in various ways, the most common being no sales allowed on Sundays. A major source of cultural (and sometimes political) conflict between Germans and Hoboken's native-born Americans and Irish was the German practice of "Continental Sunday," in which Germans drank, danced, sang, played and listened to music and held family picnics on a day that non-Germans considered to be a solemn and quiet time of church attendance and prayer. Germans' insistence on a glass of beer or wine with Sunday meals was particularly shocking to Anglo-Americans and temperance-minded Irish priests: "To the average American, the open defiance of the customs of the land, with regard to Sunday observance: the open indulgence in beer and wine in the presence of women and children, who took part in these pleasures, and to crown all this, seeming lack of interest in church matters, was nothing less than proof of total depravity."[79]

To Germans, the American hostility toward alcohol represented an attack on their culture, and they used the very American argument that alcohol consumption was a matter of personal liberty and one that government should stay out of. One reason, in fact, why Hoboken attracted so many German residents in the 1850s and 1860s, even before the German shipping lines began sailing to Hoboken, was that many German New Yorkers regularly picnicked at the Elysian Fields and liked the community enough to settle there permanently. And they brought their beer- and wine-drinking traditions with them. By 1885, Hoboken had eighty-one lager saloons and fifty-three wine and liquor stores, most of them owned by Germans.[80]

Despite their numerical majority in many communities, Germans largely failed to dominate American political institutions. Part of this was due to the fact that Germans were split between the Democratic and Republican Parties. Some Germans became alienated from the Republicans after the Civil War because of the party's support for alcohol prohibition and other Sabbath regulations, while others, particularly German Protestants, disliked the Irish domination of the Democratic Party and so voted Republican. In Hudson County, Irish American political bosses were careful to keep their German-born constituents from feeling unappreciated or ignored. "It became an unwritten rule that the most important posts of mayor of Jersey City and county supervisor were to go to a German and an Irishman."[81] In the 1860s, Frederick W. Bohnstedt served as city coroner. One of the few prominent German American politicians in Hoboken in the early twentieth century was cigar manufacturer Adolph Lankering, who served as mayor from 1901 to 1906, when President Woodrow Wilson appointed him postmaster of Hoboken, a stable and prestigious patronage job.[82] And German American Gustav Bach served on the Hoboken City Council and Board of Commissioners for many years, beginning in 1902.[83]

One area that Germans did have significant influence over was education. Beginning in the 1840s and 1850s, German émigrés were at the forefront of building schools based on the German model of clustering students according to ages and abilities. In 1854, Dr. Eduard Feldner opened a German boarding school in Hoboken, which was taken over a year later by Dr. Rudolf Dulon. Dulon's daughter taught the elementary grades, and fellow refugee Franz Sigel taught the higher grades. Exams were held in public at Hoboken's Shakespeare Hotel, and famous refugees

The primary class at the Hoboken German Academy, circa 1890. *Hoboken Historical Museum.*

such as Gustav Struve occasionally spoke to the student body. By 1857, enrollment was 250 students. Although Dulon moved to Rochester, New York, in 1866, the school survived.[84]

The most important German educator in Hoboken was Adolf Douai, the first principal of the Hoboken Academy. A Marxist revolutionary from Thuringia who immigrated to the United States in 1852, Douai wrote extensively about education, publishing a German grammar book, a phonetic primer, books about kindergarten and physical education and the philosophical work *The Idea of God*. In 1860, 250 German parents established the Hoboken Academy and hired Douai to be principal and Caroline Louise Frankenberg (who had studied with early childhood pioneer Friedrich Wilhelm August Fröbel) to organize one of the first kindergartens in the country. In February 1861, the school opened with 177 students.[85] German parents also founded the Martha Institute, headed by the Reverend Leopold Mohn of the German Evangelical Church, in 1857. By 1883, 150 students were attending the school.[86]

But German parents did not have to send their children to the German schools to maintain their language and culture. Beginning in the early 1880s, Hoboken children studied German in the public schools, beginning in the first grade, regardless of home language. Thus, many Hoboken residents who did not speak German at home became bilingual, a skill required in a community with so many German speakers, many of them recent immigrants.

Germans also maintained their native language by reading German-language newspapers. Many Hoboken Germans read the New York–based *New Yorker Zeitung* and the *New Yorker Herald*, but also the *New Jersey Staats Courier* (founded in 1851 and based in Newark), the *New Jersey Freie Zeitung* (founded in 1858) and the Jersey City–published *New Jersey Staats Zeitung*. By 1901, New Jersey had twenty-six German-language publications, most of them weekly newspapers and magazines.[87]

Unlike the Irish, who were nearly homogeneous in their Catholicism, German immigrants were Roman Catholic, Lutheran, German Reformed (Calvinist), Jewish and "freethinking" (a term used to describe anti-church intellectuals). Germans quickly built churches and synagogues in Hoboken and helped rejuvenate existing congregations with new members. By 1900, Hoboken had five German-language churches—the German Evangelical Church at 606 Garden Street (1856); St. Matthew's Lutheran Church at 57

Eighth Street (1858); St. Joseph's Roman Catholic Church at 61 Monroe Street (1874); the German Methodist Episcopal Church at 151 Garden Street (1875); and Sts. Peter and Paul Roman Catholic Church at 404 Hudson Street (1889)—and one German synagogue, Adath Emuno at 637 Garden Street (1871).[88] Hoboken also had an Orthodox synagogue, Moses Montefiore, established in 1901 and located at 76 Grand Street. That temple recruited a German-born rabbi, Chayim Hershensohn, who immigrated with his family in 1903 and lived at 322 Park Avenue.[89]

Roman Catholics were the largest religious group within Hoboken's German community; by the early twentieth century, Hoboken had between three and four thousand German Catholics. But as in New York, Hoboken's German Catholics insisted on German-language services and German Catholic traditions they had observed in Europe.[90] The idea of a German parish was strongly resisted by local priests, who insisted on ministering to all Catholics, regardless of language or national origin, despite Bishop James Roosevelt Bayley's instructions to minister only in German. St. Joseph's Church was finally

St. Matthew's German Lutheran Church, 57 Eighth Street at Hudson Street, 1877. *Hoboken Historical Museum.*

established as a German parish by the Franciscan priest Father Alphonsus Zoeller in 1874. But after Father Zoeller died in 1881, the congregation quickly dwindled to only five families. By 1884, St. Joseph's had begun to revive under the leadership of an Italian priest, Father Dominick Marzetti, who preached in English, German and Italian. St. Joseph's Parish also had a parochial school managed by the Sisters of St. Francis.[91] But as more Italian immigrants moved into the neighborhood around St. Joseph's in the 1890s, the church took on an Italian character, and German parishioners began to attend Sts. Peter and Paul, which was established as a German parish in 1889.[92]

Many other Hoboken Germans were Lutheran, and German Lutheran immigrants were initially dismayed by the American Lutheran Church, finding it to be doctrinally loose and anglicized in language and practice. "The newcomers infused new life into the Lutheran Church," reemphasizing the importance of the German language in worship and bringing strict orthodoxy to the American church.[93] The first Lutheran church in Hoboken was the German Lutheran Church of St. Matthew, which was organized in 1858. The church's first minister was the Reverend C.M. Wassidlow, a native of Pomerania, who was supported in his ministry efforts by the German Lutheran churches in New York City, St. Matthew and St. Mark. After initially failing to buy the Presbyterian church building at the corner of Third and Washington Streets, the congregation finally bought the structure in 1864 and opened a day school in the church's basement. In 1877, the congregation sold the Washington Street building for $10,000 (it had paid $6,700 in 1864) and bought a lot on the corner of Ninth and Bloomfield Streets for $8,000. But in the tradition of speculative real estate in Hoboken, the church's building committee decided to trade that lot for the land at the corner of Hudson and Eighth Streets for $14,500 and build a bigger church, with capacity to seat six hundred people. After the Reverend Wassidlow died in 1875, the Reverend Dr. Henry Hafermann was called from Germany and placed in charge of building the new church structure. After a turbulent period, Reverend Hafermann was recalled in 1880 and replaced by the Reverend Peter Erich, who also clashed with his parishioners. The congregation finally settled down in 1890 with the hiring of the Reverend Alexander Richter, who preached at St. Matthew's for many years until his death in 1914 and his replacement by the Reverend Hermann Bruckner.[94] St. Matthew's is still located at 57 Eighth Street, and its 150-foot steeple

Left: German Methodist Church, 151 Garden Street, circa 1933. *Hoboken Historical Museum.*

Below: German Evangelical Church, 606 Garden Street, circa 1920. *Hoboken Historical Museum.*

tower, complete with clock and bells, remains one of the defining landmarks on the Hoboken skyline.

Another Lutheran church, St. John the Baptist (later the Evangelical Lutheran St. John's), was organized in 1889 by several members of the Reformed Church, led by their pastor, the Reverend Freund. These parishioners bought the old Baptist Church at 300 Bloomfield Street and reorganized themselves as an Evangelical congregation. This Evangelical Lutheran church attracted many German families and had several German pastors in the late nineteenth and early twentieth centuries.[95]

Germans' dominance of the local Lutheran churches prompted Scandinavian and English-speaking Lutherans to organize their own congregations. The Scandinavians, most of them Norwegian, established Scandinavian Evangelical Trinity Lutheran Church in 1890, although the congregation continued to meet at St. Matthew's at Eighth and Hudson Streets. In 1893, they bought a small lot on the corner of Ninth and Clinton Streets and built a church and parsonage. The members, most of them working-class craftsmen, donated labor and materials to build their small church. In 1900, English-speaking Lutherans formed Holy Trinity English Evangelical Church and built the present structure at 707 Washington Street in 1913.

The religious divisions among Germans caused German speakers to fashion an ethnic identity primarily around culture and especially language. Despite the dialectical differences, the German language quickly came to be the defining characteristic of the German community, along with *Gemütlichkeit* (sociability) and *Gemeinschaft* (friendliness).

Although Germans in the United States never formed an ethnic political party, they were famous for their associations, or *Vereine*. Religious, secular, social, cultural, musical, political, regional—every kind of association that could be thought of, Germans organized.

The most widespread types of Vereine were the *Unterstützungsverein*, or sickness and death benefit society, and the *Landsmannschaften*, clubs based on region of origin. Many Landsmannschaften also provided burial funds and helped pay for funeral services. Germans also organized Masonic lodges and German American fraternal associations such as the *Vereinigte Deutscher Brüder* (the United German Brothers), the Harugari, the Templars, the *Freiheitssöhne* (Freedom Sons), the B'nai B'rith (for German Jewish men) and the Free Sons of Israel (another German Jewish organization).[96]

Hoboken Deutscher Club, 600 Hudson Street, circa 1860. *Hoboken Historical Museum.*

As early as the mid-1880s, the *Deutscher Klub* (German Club) of Hoboken was the city's premier social organization. Charles B. Brush, a civil engineer who wrote the Hoboken section of William H. Shaw's encyclopedic *History of Essex and Hudson Counties* in 1884, wrote of the German Club, "Its members are composed of the very best citizens of Hoboken, with some from New York. The individual wealth of the members of this club is, in the aggregate, probably more than that of any other German club in the United States."[97]

Dr. Rudolph Rabe, who grew up in early twentieth-century Hoboken, remembered in *The Hoboken of My Boyhood* that "society in Hoboken was predominantly German, and its activities were confined, to the most part, to the 'Deutcher Club' at Sixth and Hudson Streets, whose membership could boast the wealthiest and most influential of Hoboken's citizens." Not wanting to be outdone socially, the "purely American element of the city" opened the Columbia Club at the northeast corner of Bloomfield and Eleventh Streets.[98]

Virtually all American towns with sizeable German populations in the mid- to late nineteenth century had a *Schützen* (shooting club), and Hoboken was no exception. The lack of available space in Hoboken meant that the actual shooting range was north of the city in North Bergen. In Hoboken, the Schützen members were known for their colorful funerals, in which the deceased member was given a military-style ceremony, complete with a parade up Washington Street to Eleventh Street to the tune of Chopin's Funeral March before the mourners went to the city cemetery in North Bergen. (Hoboken was deemed too small, and the Land & Improvement Company deemed its property too valuable, to have cemeteries in Hoboken.) In turn-of-the-century Hoboken, attendees at a Schützen funeral packed into German saloons, often Duhrkoops at Eleventh and Washington Streets or a saloon owned by Frederick Schulken a few doors down, for the wake and then sang "*Ich Hat ein Kameraden*" ("I Had a Comrade") before marching back downtown.[99]

Sanger (singing) societies and *Turnvereine* (gymnastics clubs) were also enormously popular among German immigrants. The Turners, as the gymnasts were called, had been associated with both liberal and radical politics in Europe since the movement's founding in Berlin in 1811. (Opponents of Germany's many autocratic regimes engaged in gymnastics as part of their paramilitary training.) As early as 1850, there were clashes between the Turners and nativist New York gangs, with one notorious incident occurring in Hoboken in 1851:

> *In May 1851, on Pentecost Sunday, a number of German workingmen, including the followers of* [socialist revolutionary Wilhelm] *Weitling, set out from New York for a picnic in Hoboken, at which Franz Arnold and Gustav Struve were the main speakers. The latter had hardly finished his plea for renewed support of republicanism in Europe when a battle royal broke out between the picnickers and New York rowdies, resulting in one death and a number of wounded.*[100]

Up to seventy Germans were arrested, prompting the New York German community to organize itself to raise a legal defense fund and to sponsor a concert "for the benefit of the 'wounded.'" After several delays, during which nativists alleged that the picnic organizers had been advocating violent Marxist revolution, the New York prosecution dropped the case against the Germans.

After the 1851 incident, the Turners provided protection to German club members and received police protection themselves when they crossed the river over to Hoboken.[101] Tensions persisted between both German and nativists and German and Irish immigrants in New York City and the surrounding communities.[102] But New York Germans continued to flock to Hoboken for singing, music concerts, club meetings and picnics.[103]

Hoboken also had a *Sommertheater* that was very popular among New York Germans, who regularly crossed the river to take in the theatrical entertainment: "The New Jersey festival grounds were especially popular because the Jersey ferries left from docks on the side of Manhattan opposite *Kleindeutschland*, thus providing an excuse for a grand parade through the city."[104]

In 1850, members of the Society of Germans for Decisive Progress in New York celebrated a huge May Day festival in Hoboken:

> *Several thousand went over to Hoboken for the festival and only bad weather kept it from being the largest Volksfest ever held in New York. At 10 A.M. they assembled* [the Turners, the Teacher's Battalion of the Social Reformers, the Freethinkers, the Society for Decisive Progress, the Social Reform Association and the German Men's Choral Society] *at City Hall Park. They marched with two bands from the park through the city to the Hudson ferry, and again from Hoboken to the festival site.*[105]

Besides the Elysian Fields, Germans living on both sides of the river patronized the growing number of beer gardens, German restaurants and concert halls established in Hoboken in the 1860s and 1870s. A Mr. Weber built the 700-seat Germania Garden at 118 Hudson about 1863, while the 300-seat Gantzberg's Hall opened in 1867 and served as both concert facility and restaurant. The Harmonia Hall, built in 1854 with 250 seats, was owned by several music clubs.[106]

By the end of the nineteenth century, Hoboken was predominantly a German town in terms of population and culture. Germans owned a large number of both small and large businesses in the city, built and attended several churches and schools and owned, managed and frequented many important social and cultural institutions. Germans also occasionally held important local political positions, but in politics, Germans struggled to share power with Hoboken's large Irish community.

3

WHERE THE IRISH RULED

Hoboken's other large immigrant community, the Irish, was unlike the Germans in almost every way. The regional, socioeconomic and religious diversity that defined the German community did not affect the Irish, who were mostly poor or working class and almost exclusively Roman Catholic. Starting out with less education and fewer skills and resources than their fellow immigrants from Germany, Irish Hobokenites took longer to work their way up the socioeconomic ladder, but eventually these immigrants built a stable community grounded in "parish, pub, and politics." By World War I, Hoboken might have been "Little Bremen," but Irish immigrants and their children ran Hoboken politically.

Although both New York and New Jersey had Irish communities before the 1840s, most of these people were Scots-Irish Presbyterians who had emigrated from Northern Ireland before the American Revolution or soon after. Besides being Protestant like the vast majority of Americans, these early Irish immigrants were English speaking; came from more urban, industrialized areas of Ireland; or were artisans or farmers. After the Great Potato Famine of 1845–52 began, most Irish emigrants came from the rural south and west and were Roman Catholic, and many spoke Gaelic. Desperately poor cottagers (a type of sharecropping farmer), these Irish immigrants had little experience living in a modern urban, industrializing society and had experienced a traumatic migration driven by starvation and dispossession.[107]

East Coast
Southeast
Southwest
West
Midlands
Northwest
Northern Ireland

IRELAND

Most of the Irish immigrants to Hoboken came from the Irish west coast, particularly from County Mayo, with a substantial minority coming from Mayo's neighbor, County Galway, and County Kerry. County Roscommon, just east of Mayo, and County Cavan were distinctive in that they are located in central Ireland but still sent many immigrants to Hoboken. Hoboken also received significant numbers of immigrants from County Clare, on the west coast just south of Galway, and County Cork, on the southern coast.[108]

Irish immigrants settled in most areas of Hoboken, except for the wealthy Second Ward. In 1860, out of 593 Irish-born males in Hoboken, 263 lived in the First Ward, near the waterfront; 120 lived in the Second Ward; and 209 lived in the Third Ward in the western part of town (Hoboken only had three wards in 1860). In the 1870s, the Third and Fourth Wards became more Irish, as both the city and the Irish population grew. Whereas in some cities Irish immigrants clustered in certain neighborhoods, usually the poorest, the small size of Hoboken meant that Irish residents came to monopolize certain blocks or even certain multifamily buildings of ten or more families. In the 1870s, for example, the first few blocks of Ferry Street and the first blocks of Jefferson and Monroe Streets were predominantly Irish.[109]

Nineteenth-century Irish Catholics in the urban areas of New Jersey—Jersey City, Newark, etc.—lived in highly segregated working-class neighborhoods in which community life revolved around the parish church, parochial school and Irish and Catholic associations, such as the Friendly Sons of St. Patrick and the Ancient Order of Hibernians. Discriminated against by Protestant Americans and disdainful of Protestant American institutions, these Irish immigrants created a parallel world of American Catholic institutions that was "dominated by parish and pub," with the third part of the triangle being Democratic Party politics.[110]

But Irish immigrants and their American-born children were not as segregated in Hoboken as they were in larger cities. Hoboken's small geographic size meant that while there were some blocks with high Irish density, Irish immigrants and their children could be found in all parts of town, living next door to Anglo-Americans and Germans (despite some Germans' apparent antipathy toward the Irish). Although the Fourth Ward came to be known as an Irish neighborhood, the southwest part of Hoboken was never an Irish ghetto the way the Horseshoe District in Jersey City was.

Language initially composed a fourth leg of the foundation of Hoboken's Irish community. Learning Gaelic was encouraged by some Irish community leaders as a way of fostering a distinct Irish identity based on language, similar to what Germans from diverse parts of Central Europe were doing in North America. To learn Gaelic "means you will feel more proud and manly and Irishmen, and be more respected as American citizens," an Irish Hobokenite claimed.[111] In the 1870s, every major New Jersey city had at least one Gaelic school, yet Gaelic never became a defining aspect of Irish identity the way Catholicism and the aspiration of an Ireland politically independent from Great Britain did.

With large numbers of Irish immigrants settling in Hudson County in the mid- to late nineteenth century, Hoboken's Catholic population grew correspondingly. Before 1836, when St. Peter's Church was built in Jersey City, Catholics in Hudson County used to pray together in one another's homes, and priests from New York City visited to administer the sacraments when needed. In the mid-1840s, a priest from Jersey City came regularly to Hoboken to hold Mass in the Phoenix Hotel, at the corner of Washington and First Streets, which was owned by a Mrs. Sweeney. But the priest's efforts to convince the congregation to raise money for a church of its own were unsuccessful.

After much pressure from church leadership in Jersey City, a ten-year campaign to raise funds and a lengthy legal debate with the City of Hoboken,

Our Lady of Grace Church, 400 Willow Avenue, Church Square Park, circa early 1930s. *Hoboken Historical Museum.*

St. Mary's Roman Catholic Church (now Our Lady of Grace) was finally built at the corner of Willow and Fourth Streets and consecrated in July 1855. To give the new church relics, Bishop Bayley presided over the reburial of the bones of an obscure martyr, St. Quietus, at St. Mary's in June 1856, to the shock and horror of the area's many Protestants.[112] In 1858, a portrait of the Virgin Mary, donated by the Duchess of Genoa in memory of her late husband, was coronated at St. Mary's in a special ceremony overseen by Bayley and attended by a large audience of local Catholics.[113]

The construction of St. Mary's was largely the work of a French priest from Nice, Reverend Anthony Cauvin, who had been sent to Hoboken by New York Archbishop John Hughes in 1851. Before the church was built, Reverend Cauvin held Mass on weekdays in his apartment on Southeast Washington Terrace at the corner of Newark Street and was responsible for organizing Catholic congregations and building churches in West Hoboken (now Union City) and Fort Lee.[114]

Originally, St. Mary's had been intended to be built on Church Square, not fronting it, but only good legal advice kept the church and congregation from being caught in a nasty fight between the City of Hoboken and the Hoboken Land & Improvement Company (HLIC). In 1852, Reverend Cauvin applied to the Land & Improvement Company for a lot on Church Square. Hoboken's Methodist congregation had built a church there in 1846 and a Dutch Reformed church was also under construction on the northeastern corner of the square (at Garden and Fifth Streets). But the attorneys Reverend Cauvin consulted advised the priest that the square was actually public property, and thus the HLIC did not have the right to sell any lots there, nor did the church have the right to build a religious facility there either. The HLIC and the Stevens family, not surprisingly, disagreed, but by this point, the City of Hoboken was a separate legal entity from the Land & Improvement Company, and the Stevens family, though influential, did not control the city. (In 1864, the City of Hoboken successfully sued the Methodists, who had to abandon their church in 1865, when a jury ruled that the square was public space.)

To avoid being caught in the middle of the city-HLIC dispute, Reverend Cauvin bought three lots on Willow Street, fronting the square but not actually on it, for his church in 1854. He also bought the window frames from the Dutch Reformed congregation, which had abandoned the

St. Mary's Hospital, Willow Avenue, circa 1920. *Hoboken Historical Museum.*

construction of its church when the question of the legality of building on the square had arisen.[115]

With St. Mary's as an anchor, Hoboken's Irish Catholic community grew and thrived, building first a small school and a house for teacher Sarah Mahoney in 1859 and later a hospital and orphanage run by the Sisters of the Poor of St. Francis in 1863. In 1864, a parochial school run by the Sisters of Charity of Madison took over Mahoney's school, and she entered a convent in Brooklyn. Several Catholic women's societies were established in this time period, helping foster a strong lay community based around parish and parochial school, and Bishop Bayley also promoted temperance societies for both men and women.[116] In September 1864, St. Mary's changed its name to Our Lady of Grace.

At the time of the consecration of the church in 1855, St. Mary's had a congregation of about 750 people, and the congregation was both Irish and German. In 1857, when the first church census of Catholics was taken, Hoboken had 1,600 Catholics composing 300 families (at a time when the entire population of the city was 9,660).[117] In 1884, Our Lady of Grace had a congregation of approximately 6,500, and 900 children attended its Sunday school.[118] To protect Catholic children from Protestant influence and proselytizing and to further encourage parochial school enrollment, Newark bishop Winand Michael Wigger prohibited the families of children attending public school from receiving absolution.[119] "The Catholic element in Hoboken is numerous and powerful, and at the time the church of Our Lady of Grace was built it was the largest church edifice in New Jersey, while the school attached to it was said to be one of the largest parochial schools in the United States."[120]

The Catholic Church in Hoboken thrived because of the large size of the population but also because of the stable leadership of Reverend Cauvin, who served as head priest in Hoboken for twenty-two years, finally retiring and returning to France in 1873. Cauvin was first replaced by the Reverend Major Charles Duggan, an Irish priest trained in the United States, from 1873 to 1876, and then the Reverend Patrick Corrigan, an immigrant priest from Longford, Ireland, from 1876 to his death in 1896.[121] Reverend Corrigan oversaw the construction of Our Lady of Grace's current building in 1878.[122]

As in other areas where Irish immigrants settled, the Irish quickly came to dominate the local Catholic Church, both as laity and as clergy. After a generation of uneasy accommodation, major conflict between Irish and German Catholics emerged in the 1890s over the issue of the use of language outside Mass (which was, of course, in Latin), certain rituals and hymns. German Catholics, not surprisingly, wanted German-speaking priests to administer non-Mass sacraments (such as confession and Last Rites) and to maintain their European traditions, which differed from those of Irish and American Catholics. In 1890, European members of the St. Raphaelsverein, a lay society for German Catholic immigrants founded by German merchant Peter Paul Cahensly, petitioned the pope for more German bishops in the United States. This petition sparked a furor among English-speaking Catholics. Reverend Corrigan was among those local Catholic leaders who objected to "Cahenslyism," calling it a conspiracy to "Germanize the country by means of the church."[123] Corrigan's successor, the Reverend Charles J. Kelly, was also Irish American and unsympathetic to the German demands for more German priests and bishops. Complicating the controversy was the fact that the bishop of Newark at the time, Bishop

Wigger, had been born in Germany. Although Bishop Wigger did not support Cahenslyism, he did sponsor a meeting of the Society of German American Priests in Newark in 1892, angering Irish priests and further enflaming the debate, which continued until John Joseph O'Connor became bishop of Newark in 1901.[124] Resentful Irish Catholics also remembered how Bishop Bayley had promoted the formation of St. Joseph's as a German parish in the early 1870s, repeatedly dismissing priests who persisted in preaching in English instead of German, and how Sts. Peter and Paul had been established for Germans in 1889.[125]

Although the Catholic Church began to appoint German-speaking priests to German congregations in the late nineteenth century, the main focus of American Catholic leaders was to try to Americanize and integrate German Catholics into the Irish-dominated church. The Germans' fight to have German-language parishes led the way for Italians, Poles and other non-English-speaking Catholics to petition for their own national and linguistic parishes to maintain their groups' particular flavors of Catholicism.

Irish priests such as Reverend Corrigan were respected by their Irish congregations because they also confronted the same challenges their parishioners faced in living in an often hostile American Protestant society. The one area in which Irish priests had little influence, however, was over Irish American drinking habits. The stereotype of the drunken Irishman was a product of the Irish immigrant experience in the United States; few Irish peasants could afford to drink as much as Irish immigrants and Irish Americans did in America. The Irish pub, with its traditions of food and sociability, gave way in the American context to the saloon, where beer and hard liquor flowed and mixed with local politics. Despite the regular and earnest preaching by priests and the establishment of several temperance organizations, Irish bars and Irish drinking flourished in American cities, including Hoboken.

In the mid-nineteenth century, Irish immigrant men were primarily customers, not owners, of saloons in Hoboken. In 1860, out of 593 Irish-born men, only three were saloon or bar keepers and three were hotel owners (all hotels also had bars and often restaurants). These businessmen were among the community's more prosperous members, and all three of the hoteliers—forty-year-old Bernard Lougher, thirty-one-year-old Michael Murphey and twenty-eight-year-old Robert Nicle—lived in the upper-middle-class Second Ward and had between $500 and $1,000 worth of personal property. Thirty-year-old liquor dealer William Spooner also lived in the Second Ward.[126]

In the 1880s, most Hoboken saloons continued to be owned by Germans. This made the few Irish bar owners important members of their community. Daniel Donegan, who was born in Ireland in 1847 at the height of the famine, owned a saloon at 408 Clinton Street and lived with his sister, Joanna, and brother-in-law, Edward McSerceney, a brick layer, on the west side of Clinton (possibly next door to or above the bar).[127] In 1884, Thomas F. Normoyle owned a saloon at 187 Willow Avenue and another place at 514 Fourth Street in 1891 but by 1910 had become a groundskeeper for the City of Hoboken.[128]

But in the 1890s, the Irish became competitive in the Hoboken liquor business. Of the 240 restaurant and saloon owners in Hoboken in 1895, nearly 30 had Irish-sounding surnames, such as Brennan, Byrne, Callahan, Kelly, McLaughlin, O'Connor and Sheehan.[129]

The saloon was the major site of political activity for naturalized immigrants and native-born Americans of all ethnic and religious backgrounds in the nineteenth century. Saloons provided an easy and gender-exclusive environment in which (male) voters could socialize, and many bar keepers were prominent in local political party organizations.

Arriving in New York with no intention of returning to a devastated, starving Ireland, Irish immigrants embraced life in America. They quickly found a welcome home in the Democratic Party. The Democratic Party had long attracted libertarian-minded Americans, who were put off by the Whig Party's willingness to interfere in affairs of personal morality, particularly temperance, Sabbath regulations and slavery. The Democrats also gained the support of many immigrants offended by the nativism of the American or Know-Nothing Party. By the time the Republican Party had emerged in the mid-1850s, Irish Americans had joined the Democratic Party in full force, thanks to political parties' control of the naturalization process, particularly in urban areas. New Jersey's large Irish immigrant population caused it to be one of only three states to vote for Democratic presidential candidate General George McClellan in 1864. (McClellan was, of course, defeated by President Abraham Lincoln.)

Irish American attorney Leon Abbett, who moved to Hoboken from Philadelphia in 1862, quickly became a leader in the Hudson County Democratic Party, riding McClellan's coattails to Trenton and serving as a state assemblyman representing Hoboken and Weehawken from 1864 to 1866 (and again from 1869 to 1870). He was also Hoboken's corporation attorney, the city's chief legal official, in the mid-1860s. According to historian Dermot Quinn, "Abbett had an unusually acute instinct that the appeal most likely to succeed in Hudson County was to ethnic fear."[130] He knew that Irish immigrants saw themselves in economic competition with African Americans (despite Hudson County's tiny number of blacks), and so he and other Civil War–era Democrats regularly made blatant anti-black appeals to Irish American voters. In his 1864 campaign, Abbett quickly staked out a strong position against any Civil War–related proposals from the Republican Party: opposition to the draft; to integrating black Americans into full political citizenship; to giving equal pensions to war widows, regardless of race; to giving Union soldiers the right to vote in the field; and even to acknowledging Lincoln's role in preserving the Union. After the war, Abbett had a long and distinguished political career, serving in the New Jersey State Senate (from 1875 to 1877), as governor of New Jersey (from 1884 to 1887 and 1890 to 1893) and on the State Supreme Court (from 1893 to 1894) before he died in 1894.[131] Irish American support for leaders such as Abbett ensured that New Jersey would be dominated by the Democratic Party for much of the postbellum period.

Despite their antipathy to African Americans, the Irish in Hoboken fought for the Union army in large numbers. Of the 177 Hoboken men who served in a volunteer regiment, most had Irish names, such as Dolan, Dugan, Doyle, Kennedy, McCarthy, Murphy, O'Brien and Sullivan.

In the post–Civil War period, Hoboken became part of a larger, Irish-dominated Democratic organization that was based in Jersey City and governed Hudson County: "In the 1880s, Dennis McLaughlin, John Feeny, Patrick H. Neill, and Robert Davis, constituted the "Big Four" who ruled Jersey City…During their reign, Hudson County was wide open with gambling houses, brothels, and saloons doing business seven days a week."[132] In the 1890s, Irish American James Smith Jr. of Newark was the "Big Boss" of New Jersey Democrats. Smith handpicked the state's Democratic gubernatorial candidates from 1895 to 1910, when Woodrow Wilson became governor.[133]

Although the Catholic Church, entrepreneurship and politics provided avenues for Irish residents to move up into the middle class, Hoboken's Irish community, as in the rest of Hudson County and the state, was predominantly working-class until the early twentieth century, when a small middle class descended from Hoboken's first Irish immigrants emerged.

Given their general poverty and the famine that caused many Irish to emigrate, it is not surprising that the majority of Irish-born men in Hoboken in 1850 were laborers. But there were also Irish blacksmiths, carpenters, butchers, shoemakers and bakers, including one who reported property worth $10,000. Among the professional classes, Hoboken had an Irish lawyer, three Irish merchants and six Irish clerks in 1850. There were also as many Irish-born men as Germans working as skilled artisans.[134]

A decade later, 40 percent of the town's 548 adult Irish men over the age of fifteen worked as laborers, but the number of clerks had jumped significantly, from 6 in 1850 to 46 in 1860. Irish men continued to have limited occupational diversity when compared to German and English immigrants. After laborer, the most commonly named occupations for Irish males in the census of 1860 were carpenter, baker, blacksmith and tailor.

An Old Hunker Fishing for Votes. "A lithograph designed and published by H.R. Robinson, 31 Park Row, N.Y. (adjoining Lovejoy's Hotel), 1848." *Library of Congress.*

But Hoboken's Irish community had increased its overall wealth, especially in real estate holdings, between 1850 and 1860. Although there were still a large number of men with personal property worth less than $100, there were also a handful of very wealthy Irishmen who identified themselves as either being a "gentleman" (meaning wealthy enough to not have to work) or having no occupation. Of the 548 Irishmen fifteen years and older listed in the census of 1860, 149 were identified as having either real estate or personal property. Of these, 19 Irish-born men had real estate holdings worth $5,000 or more, including fifty-one-year-old William White, a Second Ward resident who listed his occupation as "gentleman" and claimed real estate worth $45,000 and a personal estate of $40,000; forty-eight-year-old baker Peter McHan, who said he had $25,000 in real estate (probably his bakery) and lived in the First Ward; fifty-one-year-old James Curran, who reported owning real estate worth $20,000 and also lived in the First Ward; forty-year-old John Walker, an engineer in the Second Ward who claimed to have $12,000 worth of real estate and $2,000 in personal property; sixty-four-year-old gentleman Andrew McWorton, who lived in the Second Ward and had real estate worth $9,000 and a personal estate of $10,000; and seventy-year-old James Miller, who also lived in the Second Ward and claimed real estate worth $15,000.

Some tradesmen also did well financially. Two grocers living in the First Ward, twenty-four-year-old John Sullivan and twenty-seven-year-old John Ryan, reported that they owned real estate worth $8,000 and $5,000, respectively, and Sullivan also had $1,000 in personal property. Forty-year-old huckster John McGovern reported having real estate worth $10,000 and a personal estate of $10,000. McGovern lived in the wealthier Second Ward on a block of mostly German merchants. William Redman, a forty-five-year-old blacksmith also living in the Second Ward, had real estate worth $10,000 but only $150 in personal property; most of his wealth was probably in his forge. A fifty-year-old machinist living in the Second Ward, James Tallon, was in a similar situation. He reported owning real estate worth $8,000 but personal property of only $500. Other successful Irish-born businessmen were thirty-two-year-old druggist Francis Johnson, a resident of the Third Ward, and thirty-year-old dry goods clerk Franklin J. Rockwell, a resident of the Second Ward; both Johnson and Rockwell reported owning real estate worth $5,000, and Rockwell reported a personal estate worth $2,000. Fifty-five-year-old mariner Peter Carrigan, a resident of the First Ward, had real estate worth $7,000 and personal property worth $4,000.[135]

Approximately 50 percent of Irish immigrants to New Jersey were employed as laborers or domestic servants in 1880, but by 1900

> *the Irish recorded more lawyers and government officials than any other nationality, were well represented among the journalists, and equaled the British in number of clergymen. There were also numerous clerks, bookkeepers, merchants, bank officials, salesmen, and manufacturers of Irish stock, but they were, on the whole, not in the proportion of the Irish stock to the total labor force. In the area of public employment as policemen and firemen, the Irish far outdistanced all other nationalities.[136]*

Irish Americans' progression up the socioeconomic ladder was slower than that of German Americans and emerged primarily through the public sector and the Catholic Church. But they did rise, as Catholic institutions and local Democratic Party politics provided new opportunities for education, professional networks and business entrepreneurship.

Although the Irish and Germans achieved socioeconomic success and political power in Hoboken in different ways, together these two groups defined Hoboken community life in ways that the English, Dutch and Scandinavians did not. It would take decades and several accidents of history for later immigrant groups to dislodge the Germans and Irish from their commanding positions. In the early twentieth century, these new immigrants faced similar challenges of settlement and adjustment to those faced by Hoboken's first immigrants in the mid-nineteenth century.

4

HOBOKEN AND THE FEDERAL
IMMIGRATION SYSTEM,
1892–1917

For most of the nineteenth century, the federal government played almost no role in regulating immigration beyond requiring the Department of State to collect statistics from the ports about the numbers and origins of new arrivals (land border crossings from Canada and Mexico were largely ignored until the Naturalization Act of 1906). In 1867, the responsibility for collecting statistics about immigration was moved from the State Department to the Bureau of Statistics in the Treasury Department primarily because the Treasury Department had greater data collection and analysis capacity. In 1875, the federal government took its first steps toward regulating immigration after the Supreme Court ruled in *Henderson v. Mayor of New York* that state laws, such as the ones creating and governing the New York Board of Commissioners of Emigration (and specifically, the head tax the commission charged), were unconstitutional because they usurped Congress's exclusive power to regulate foreign commerce.[137] Yet beyond declaring that the emigration commissioners were illegally regulating foreign commerce by charging a head tax on each immigrant arrival, the federal government was still reluctant to take control of the nation's immigration policy. The federal government created a list of unworthy types to exclude (prostitutes in 1875; the insane, the retarded and those "liable to become a public charge" in 1882; and contract laborers in 1885); restricted immigration from China (in 1882); and required steamship companies to pay for the cost of returning

Immigrants walk up the boardwalk from the barge that ferried them to Ellis Island from the steamship company's docks. Originally published in *Quarantine Sketches* (Maltine Company, 1902, p. 25). *Library of Congress.*

inadmissible aliens (also in 1882) but left the enforcement of these new laws in the hands of the states.

In 1891, Congress finally passed the Immigration Act of 1891, making the federal government responsible for immigration policy and adding to the exclusion list polygamists, persons convicted of "crimes involving moral turpitude" and persons suffering from "a loathsome or contagious disease."[138] To inspect new arrivals, the Treasury Department, which was responsible for implementing the new legislation, opened several immigration stations, including the nation's largest and most famous, Ellis Island in New York Harbor, in 1892.

It was fitting that the Treasury Department should be responsible for immigration at the turn of the twentieth century because federal immigration policy was primarily concerned with excluding a small but growing list of undesirables (including Chinese) and with collecting the immigrant head tax, which was one dollar in 1894, two dollars in 1903, four dollars in 1907 and eight dollars in 1917. With hundreds of thousands of immigrants entering the United States every year before World War I, immigration was literally a very

Holland American docks, circa 1900–15. *Library of Congress, Prints & Photographs Division, Detroit Publishing Company Collection (reproduction number LC-D4-15659 L [b&w glass neg]).*

profitable moneymaking venture for the federal government. States like New York and New Jersey occasionally demanded a share of the head tax revenue, since they bore the social costs of immigration, but the federal government dismissed these claims, and the money flowed directly into the federal coffers.[139]

Immigration became big business in Hoboken during this period as well, as hundreds of thousands of immigrant travelers often first set foot on American soil on one of Hoboken's piers. Immigration was the lifeblood of the Port of New York, as well as of Hoboken's many waterfront hotels, restaurants and saloons. Four of the five shipping lines with piers in Hoboken catered to passenger travel, and dozens of cabdrivers and luggage porters and the hundreds of others who worked for the shipping companies also depended on immigration and immigrants for their livelihoods. And like everything else in America in the late nineteenth and early twentieth centuries, competition for this immigrant travel business was fierce and freewheeling.

Hoboken and the Federal Immigration System, 1892–1917

By the turn of the twentieth century, the actual travel experience of immigration had become much easier, safer and more comfortable for people. In 1890, the Hamburg-America line set an international speed record for crossing the Atlantic from London to Hoboken in just under seven days.[140] The cost of a steerage ticket was approximately twenty-five dollars (depending on the departure and arrival ports).[141] The great ocean liners that began arriving and departing from Hoboken several times per week in the 1890s and early 1900s had luxurious furnishings, haute cuisine and attentive service—for those who could afford to pay the cost of a first-class ticket. Those who could not had to content themselves with fast passage across the ocean. But third-class passengers did have some degree of privacy and cleanliness that the steerage passengers of the mid-nineteenth century did not.

By the early twentieth century, increasingly large and luxurious liners were regularly docking along Hoboken's piers. The arrival or departure of a new ship on its maiden voyage was an event on both sides of the Atlantic, and Hoboken residents regularly crowded the piers to welcome or bid farewell to the latest model.[142] An event like the June 30, 1900 fire that killed more than three hundred people and destroyed most of the North German Lloyd pier facilities, including the SS *Bremen*, was not just a tragedy for the German shipping company but also an experience that was deeply felt by all Hobokenites.[143]

After a steamship docked at one of the Manhattan or Hoboken piers, first- and second-class passengers were interviewed by immigration authorities onboard ship before disembarking at the Barge Office on Whitehall Street at the eastern end of Manhattan's Battery Park. Upper-class passengers traveling on the German, Dutch or Scandinavian lines could take the ferry from Hoboken to Manhattan or catch a train west to their ultimate destinations. After first- and second-class passengers were off ship, steerage and third-class passengers were ferried to Ellis Island for inspection by immigration authorities.[144]

At Ellis Island, would-be immigrants experienced an efficient and impersonal inspection process in which literally thousands of people could be examined by doctors and government inspectors in one day.

American sociologist Edward A. Steiner sailed from Europe to New York in 1906, posing as an immigrant to observe conditions at Ellis Island and the implementation of federal immigration regulations. He described the process:

The barges on which the immigrants are towed towards the island are of a somewhat antiquated pattern and if I remember rightly have done service in the Castle Garden days, and before that some of them at least had done full service for excursion parties up and down Long Island Sound. The structure towards which we sail and which gradually rises from the surrounding sea is rather imposing, and impresses one by its utilitarian dignity and by its plainly expressed official character.

With tickets fastened to our caps and to the dresses of the women, and with our own bills of lading in our trembling hands, we pass between rows of uniformed attendants, and under the huge portal of the vast hall where the final judgment awaits us. We are cheered somewhat by the fact that assistance is promised to most of us by the agents of various National Immigrant Societies who seem both watchful and efficient.

Mechanically and with quick movements we are examined for general physical defects and for the dreaded trachoma, an eye disease, the prevalence of which is greater in the imagination of some statisticians than it is on board immigrant vessels.

From here we pass into passageways made by iron railings, in which only lately, through the intervention of a humane official, benches have been placed, upon which, closely crowded, we await our passing before the inspectors.[145]

Crying babies, lost children, anxious people and overworked inspectors, translators and doctors—Ellis Island was a place of great emotional stress.

Yet, despite this, the rejection rate at Ellis Island and other U.S. immigration stations was very low, only 2 or 3 percent on average in any given year before World War I, or about 18,000 foreigners excluded per year out of an average of about 880,000 entrants per year between 1900 and 1910.[146] The reason for this was the steamship companies had developed extensive screening procedures at their pier facilities in Europe to avoid having to pay the cost of returning an excluded immigrant:

After quarantine and customs procedures immigrants were hustled past doctors, and a matron who examined pregnant women, on an assembly-line basis, each doctor assigned to look for one specific disease; three special inspectors decided on the doubtful cases. As health regulations were added to the exclusion clauses, the examinations grew more complex and time-

consuming. Those who passed were then interviewed by registry clerks who recorded vital statistics and other background information. Finally, the immigrants were sent to special offices housed in the federal station for currency exchange, rail tickets, baggage handling, and telegrams.[147]

From Ellis Island, newly admitted immigrants could take ferries to either the Barge Office at Battery Park in Manhattan or to Hoboken or Jersey City to catch trains west or to meet family or friends.

Immigration to the United States surged in the late nineteenth and early twentieth centuries as people were both pushed out of Europe by poverty and political instability and pulled by the economic opportunities created by American capitalism's insatiable appetite for cheap labor. By 1910, immigrants were entering New York in record numbers: 1 million entrants each year in 1905, 1906, 1907 and 1910. The average number of immigrants coming to the United States between 1900 and 1910 was 880,000 people.

Such high levels of immigration, most of it through the Port of New York, meant that conditions at Manhattan's and Hoboken's piers became increasingly chaotic. After the 1875 *Henderson v. Mayor of New York* case,

"The Hoboken Fire Katastophe." A postcard of the June 30, 1900 pier fire, with the SS *Bremen* and the SS *Main* labeled. *Hoboken Historical Museum.*

the New York Board of Commissioners of Emigration stopped regulating conditions at Castle Garden and the Battery. When the federal government opened Ellis Island in 1892, it provided no services for immigrants beyond the immigration station, nor did it regulate the hundreds of luggage porters, teamsters, hoteliers and others trying to sell their services to new arrivals in New York and Hoboken.

The growing number of immigrants and the many stories of their abuse on both sides of the river caused middle- and upper-class New York and New Jersey residents to organize pro-immigrant organizations to investigate the experiences of immigrants arriving in New York and New Jersey. These progressive reformers joined the many immigrant and religious societies that provided aid to newly arrived immigrants in the New York City area.

In 1911, in response to pressure from the pro-immigrant North American Civic League for Immigrants (NACL), the State of New Jersey created an Immigration Commission, similar to one that had been created in New York in 1910 (the NACL had been instrumental in getting that agency, the Bureau of Industries and Immigration, established as well). William Fellowes Morgan of Short Hills, New Jersey, was the chair; Robert A. Franks, Andrew Carnegie's business secretary and head of the Hudson Trust Company of Hoboken, was the secretary and treasurer; and Robert L. Fleming of Jersey City was the third member. Jersey City resident Alexander Cleland was the executive secretary. Although the legislation proposing the commission included an appropriation of $5,000, the legislature provided no actual funding, so the agency was dependent on private donations, most of which came from the NACL and such prominent businessmen as Carnegie, John D. Rockefeller, Richard Stevens and the Colgate family.[148]

Like the New York Bureau of Industries and Immigration, the New Jersey Immigration Commission investigated conditions under which immigrants traveled, lived and worked in the state. Working closely with its sponsor, the NACL's New York–New Jersey Committee, the Immigration Commission paid particular attention to conditions at the docks in Hoboken and Jersey City. And the commission members were not pleased by what they found in Hoboken.

One commission concern involved second-class passengers, more than fifty-six thousand of whom arrived in Hoboken in 1911. These passengers were "exposed to serious inconveniences because of the misleading information of porters representing immigrant hotels, and to exploitation, both by licensed porters and hackmen and by a large number of unlicensed porters and crooks," claimed the immigration commissioners.[149]

Hoboken city law required public porters (also known as city guides or runners) to be licensed, which cost $20.50 (a significant fee in 1911), and to be American citizens. Although hotels had to be licensed, hotel porters did not have to be. Public porters helped travelers with their luggage and often guided them to train or ferry terminals or wherever they wanted to go. An investigation of porters in Hoboken by the North American Civic League for Immigrants in 1911 found that many public porters lent their licenses to friends, there was no character reference for applicants to be public porters and many porters handling luggage were not licensed at all. In addition, the NACL found routine overcharging for the carrying of luggage from the piers to the Lackawanna rail or ferry terminals, as well as the practice of charging additional fees for services already included in the traveler's steamship or rail ticket price (such as shipping luggage or charging for "overweight" luggage).[150]

Unlike public porters, who were freelancers, hotel porters worked for a hotel and were responsible for recruiting guests. As in New York, Hoboken's hotel porters were aggressive in their efforts to drum up business for their employers. The commissioners scolded:

> *Hotel porters make a practice to meet steamers, secure groups of immigrants destined for points West and take them to the hotel with the assurance that no trains are leaving for their destination until the next day. In many cases it would have been possible for the immigrants to have taken a train within an hour of their arrival at Hoboken. Those guilty of this extortion count upon the ignorance of their victims who are frequently unaware of the fraud that is being practiced upon them until they have reached their destination and have talked with their friends.*[151]

More serious in the eyes of the middle-class NACL investigators were the attempts (sometimes successful) by some hotel porters to seduce young women traveling alone through Hoboken. In one instance:

> *An agent of this Commission stopping at a hotel for which he* [the porter] *worked was mistaken for an emigrant girl. The porter made the*

acquaintance of this agent and tried to persuade her to go with him to New York City for immoral purposes. Failing in this he urged her on the evening following to spend the night with him at a nearby hotel. At this hotel the porter went so far as to sign his name followed by the words "and wife," before the agent disclosed her identity.[152]

Hansom cab drivers were also viewed as a problem by the Immigration Commission and the NACL. Approximately thirty-five cabbies were licensed in Hoboken, and this license required "good moral character" and adequate equipment of horse and carriage. Although there was no set rate, the accepted fare was one dollar within town, three dollars to the Erie and Pennsylvania stations in Jersey City and between four and eight dollars to different parts of New York City. However, the commissioners documented extensive overcharging (up to sixty dollars to go from the Scandinavian line pier to the Lackawanna Station, a distance of five blocks).[153]

Then there were the problems of confidence men exchanging European currency for counterfeit dollar bills; "exploiters standing on the docks and

A postcard of Busch's Hotel, Hudson at Third Street, date unknown. *Library of Congress.*

pretending to be health officers, demand[ing] fees of fifty cents to $1, or representing themselves as Customs House officials, charg[ing] fees for 'passing baggage through,'"; pickpockets; and other thieves.[154]

Since the majority of people traveling through New York were foreigners, entrepreneurs opened "immigrant hotels," also called lodging or transfer houses, that catered to immigrants and provided a variety of services beyond simply a bed for the night: food and drink, including box lunches for long train trips; luggage storage and transport to the rail or steamship terminal; steamship and train ticket sales; currency exchange and other banking services; and even the sale of American-style clothing to "green aliens

MORRIS BAUMAN, Pres.   Telephone 687 Hoboken

CONTINENTAL HOTEL & PASSENGER TRANSFER CO.

101 HUDSON STREET,

Cor. First Stree,   HOBOKEN, N. J.

NEWLY FURNISHED AND RENOVATED

UNDER NEW MANAGEMENT

UNDER NEW MANAGEMENT

CONTINENTAL

THE PERFECT HOME for EUROPEAN TRAVELERS

OPPOSITE THE PIERS OF:

Hamburg-American Line   North German Lloyd
Holland-Amerika Line
and within 10 MINUTES WALK of the
Scandinavian American Line.
The Cunard, White Star, Red Star, American, French
and Anchor Line Piers are reached within 15 MINUTES.
The Terminals of the
Delaware Lackawanna & Western, Erie, Lehigh Valley,
Pennsylvania Railroads are within 2 to 10 MINUTES.
of the Hotel.
The Pennsylvania, New York Central and Baltimore
Ohio R. R. Terminals are reached within 20 MINUTES.
(OVER)

An advertising card for the Continental Hotel & Passenger Transfer Company, 101 Hudson Street, circa 1910–14. *Hoboken Historical Museum.*

desiring to acquire an American appearance."[155] Hoboken had twenty-two hotels in the days before World War I, including the Central, the Continental, the Grand, the Germania, the Hansa, the Hudson and Meyers Hotel. The Germania, the Hansa and Meyers all catered to German speakers.

Despite the problems documented by the Immigration Commission, hotel porters and runners did provide useful services to many immigrant travelers. Continental Hotel owner Joseph Samperi emigrated from Italy as a child with his parents in 1897. He began his hotel career as a janitor before working his way up to being a bus boy, a room clerk and, finally, a porter in the 1910s. His son Paul recollected:

> *Now what does a runner do? He goes down to the steamship lines, and he mentions to the people coming in who he is and what hotel he represents, and "Would they like to stay at the hotel?" Most of them would stay a day or two at the hotel, then they would get tickets on railroads going out west. A lot of the Germans went to cities out west and to farms out west. So he would go to the German lines, the Holland line, and he would tell him, "I'm from so-and-so hotel." First it was the Central, then it was the Grand, then it was the Meyers. "We'd like to have you. We'll take care of all your needs. If you'd like us to get you tickets, to anywhere in the United States, we'll be glad to take care of you."[156]*

Although Italian born, Joseph Samperi learned German well enough to pass as German, a talent that served him well in such a predominantly German community as Hoboken.

Although one would imagine that most immigrant traffic started at the Battery and moved north and west, there was actually a seasonal nature to the flow of people through the Port of New York. Nearly as many people left New York City as entered it, particularly during the winter holiday months, and fraud and theft plagued both west- and eastbound traffic. A common practice of hotel runners affecting eastbound traffic was to force the Europe-bound traveler to stop at a hotel on his way to the pier whether or not he needed to stay overnight. Hoboken, Jersey City and New York City hotel owners often paid steamship ticket agents to direct their emigrant customers to them. Some steamship agents used the tactic of mailing the ticket directly to the hotel, forcing the traveler to go to the

Duke's House, Hudson Place and Ferry Street, circa 1903–04. *Hoboken Historical Museum.*

hotel before going to the pier, in order that the innkeeper might have the opportunity to persuade the immigrant to stay overnight, have a meal or demand a fee for holding the ticket.[157]

An alternate tactic of steamship agents was to sell a ticket that (supposedly) covered all transportation costs to Europe, including train fare to the steamship pier in Hoboken and in Europe and conveyance to a hotel in Hoboken. According to the New Jersey Immigration Commission:

> *When he* [the emigrant traveler] *arrives at the station he is met by a porter and taken to a hotel. His ticket is then taken from him, as the representative of the hotel is supposed to get it stamped by the steamship company in order to reserve a place on the steamer. The following morning the emigrant is asked to pay for his lodging and meals; and if he objects, his ticket is held, and he must either comply or lose his steamer. Often his baggage check is also retained by the hotel, which thereby gets an extra hold on him.*[158]

Joseph Samperi also worked as a tour guide in New York City for immigrants returning home to Europe. His son remembered:

> *Then there was also a stream of people going back to Europe. They had been* [in the United States] *since the 1880s or maybe even earlier, they had made their money, now they wanted to go back to Germany and live a nice life in their old hometown. A lot of these people who were going back to Europe would want to see America first. They'd never seen New York, or they'd never seen any of the important things there, so he would act as a guide, on his time off. He would take them to New York, and, of course, they tipped him.*
>
> [And then,] *a lot of them would say, "Well, gee, maybe I should get some new clothes to take with me," so he'd take them over to Geismar's* [clothing store on Washington Street in Hoboken,] *and Geismar would give him a commission on whatever he brought in.*[159]

Immigration was big business in Hoboken, and national or ethnic loyalties rarely protected the greenhorn who was passing through town. But an important minority of these immigrants were coming to Hoboken to stay, and they found themselves in a dynamic and thriving city of Germans, Irish, English, Scandinavians, Dutch and others. In the late nineteenth and early twentieth centuries, new groups began to settle in Hoboken, particularly immigrants from Italy, Russia and the Slavic parts of the Austro-Hungarian Empire. Germans, Irish, Norwegians and Dutch continued to come to Hoboken, but simply in smaller numbers. This steady steam of newcomers enriched existing immigrant communities and ensured that Hoboken's fortunes would continue to be tied to immigration, the port and the shipping industry.

The "New Immigration" to Hoboken

Italians, Slavs, Russians and Scandinavians, 1880–1917

In the 1880s, immigration to the United States began to change, both in numbers of entrants and their origins. Immigration from Germany, Ireland and Great Britain slackened and was surpassed by a dramatic increase in immigration from Southern and Eastern Europe, particularly Austria-Hungary, Italy and Russia. Although New York City received large numbers of immigrants from all of these countries, Hoboken received more immigrants from Italy than from any other nation. Slavs from Austria-Hungary, Russians and Scandinavians also settled in Hoboken, but in smaller numbers. These groups developed their own communities with their own institutions but under the shadow of the German-Irish-Italian trifecta.

In 1880, Hoboken had only 280 Italian-born residents, but that number jumped to 790 in 1890 and 2,360 in 1900. By 1910, Italian immigrants and their children were the second largest ethnic group in Hoboken after Germans. Hoboken's Italian immigrants settled into a town built by Irish labor and dominated socially and economically by Germans and Anglo-Americans. Italians moved into the unskilled laboring jobs that the Irish had held in the mid-nineteenth century and remained at the bottom of the socioeconomic totem pole until the 1920s, when the second generation began moving into skilled trade positions. But it would not be until after the Second World War that Italian Americans gained political power in Hoboken.

The few Italians who settled in Hoboken in the 1850s and 1860s were middle-class professionals, entrepreneurs or skilled artisans: clerks, brokers, printers, cabinetmakers, grocery store owners and saloonkeepers. Nearly all came to Hoboken with their families, and most owned real estate worth between $2,000 and $15,000. Out of the seven Italian-born men identified in the census of 1860, three lived in the wealthy Second Ward with their families. Catholic priests Fathers Innenlines de Conilen and Joseph Paganin were among the few Italian men who were single and did not own property. In 1870, no Italians lived in the Second Ward; instead, the tiny Italian community was almost evenly distributed between the Third and Fourth Wards in the western part of town.[160] There they worshipped at St. Joseph's Catholic Church with Germans and Irish, and their children attended the church's parochial school if their parents could afford it. This small Italian community was quickly absorbed by the thousands of poor southern Italians who came to Hoboken beginning in the 1890s.

Italians first started immigrating to the United States in large numbers in the 1890s and early 1900s. The high point of Italian immigration to the United States was 1913, when more than 870,000 people left Italy, many of them destined for America. In Hoboken, Italian immigration surged in the 1890s; within a decade, Italians were the third largest immigrant group in the city, after Germans and Irish, surpassing immigrants from Great Britain and English-speaking Canada.[161]

Italian migration at the turn of the twentieth century was distinctive from other European groups in several ways. It was predominantly male and often temporary, with most immigrants being young men coming to America to work and save enough money for their families back home to buy land, build a house or start a business. For those Italians who stayed in the United States, family members often came one by one and after the pioneering family member had spent considerable time in America. The Hoboken Italian community was a mix of single men, married men living without their families and married men living with their families, although there were more Italian men than Italian women overall between 1890 and 1920.

After Italy unified in 1871, living conditions for the peasantry worsened as the central government in Rome began treating the southern provinces as colonies to be exploited for the industrial development of the north. The combination of economic discrimination, deteriorating soil quality and

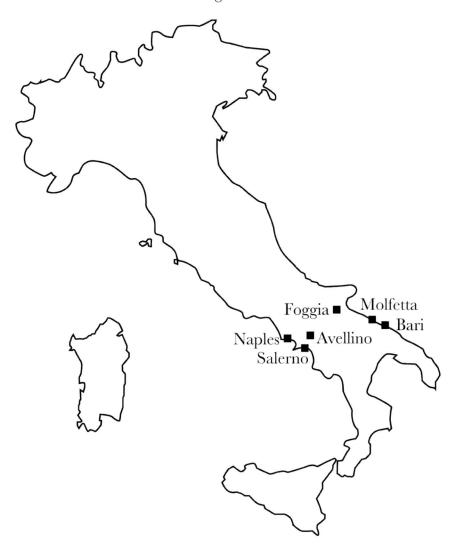

Italy.

overpopulation caused many southern Italian peasant farmers to consider emigration or at least seasonal work abroad. By the 1890s, the cheapest steamship tickets were to the United States (Brazil and Argentina had been popular migration destinations for northern Italians in the 1870s and 1880s), and so it was to America that the southern Italians went. The Hamburg-America line sailed from Naples and Genoa to New York and probably brought many Italians to Hoboken.

Unlike the Germans, who came from all German-speaking parts of Europe, many of Hoboken's Italian immigrants came from the southeast regions of Puglia and Molise. The village to send the most Italian immigrants and the one that most influenced Italian American culture in Hoboken was Molfetta, a coastal village just north of Bari. Immigrants from Foggia

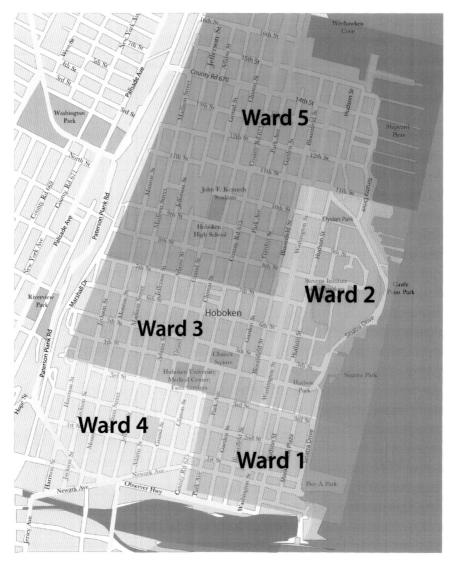

Hoboken wards, circa 1900–70.

and Avellino also settled in Hoboken in the 1910s and 1920s.[162] Although Molfetta and Avellino are not near one another, the fact that both towns sent numerous residents to Hoboken is evidence of the separate chains of migration each town in Italy established with the United States.

Most of these Italian immigrants to Hoboken settled in the Third and Fourth Wards. By 1910, the Third Ward was the Italian neighborhood, with two-thirds of Italian-born residents living in that area and the rest living in the Fourth Ward.[163] These "downtown" wards were already densely packed with tenements housing working-class immigrants and their children.

TABLE 9. ITALIANS AND THEIR U.S.-BORN CHILDREN, 1890–1930

Year	Total Population	Italian born	Native born to Italian parents	Italians as % of population
1890	43,648	790	497	3
1900	59,364	2,360	4,301	11
1910	70,324	6,555	4,727	16
1920	68,166	7,255	N/A	N/A
1930	59,261	N/A	10,716	N/A

(U.S. Census)

Italian immigrants in the early twentieth century were predominantly unskilled laborers, unlike their co-nationals, who had immigrated earlier. In 1880, the primary occupations listed by Hoboken Italians in the U.S. Census were laborer, huckster (a pushcart salesman, usually selling fruit or vegetables), grocer and carpenter. But as the decades progressed, Italians moved into two areas of work: construction (particularly bricklaying and stone cutting) and petty entrepreneurship (barbers, bakers, tailors, shoemakers and grocers) to the growing Italian community. "By 1900, the number of Italian barbers and shoemakers almost equaled that of the Germans, and within a few years the Italians had a near monopoly of these crafts."[164] One of the many small Italian businesses started in this period was Carlo's Bakery (now at 95 Washington Street, originally at 463 Fifth Street and then 212 Grand Street), which first opened in 1910. Carlo's Bakery, which was originally named Carlo Guastaferro Italian-French Pastry for its immigrant founder, was one of nineteen bakeries owned by Italians in 1915, serving the Italian community in the Third and Fourth Wards.[165] Another Italian confectioner in Hoboken, Italo Marcioni, invented the ice cream cone in 1896 and patented the mold for his unique cookie design in 1903.[166]

It was during this time that Hoboken experienced its greatest amount of physical growth, with the city adding 6,570 new buildings between 1890 and 1899 and another 3,015 structures between 1900 and 1909.[167]All of this construction, mostly brownstones being built in the northern part of the city, provided work for Hoboken's growing number of Italian construction workers.

TABLE 10. NUMBER OF HOUSING UNITS BUILT IN HOBOKEN BY DECADE

YEARS	NEW HOUSING UNITS BUILT
Before 1890	5,254
1890–1899	6,570
1900–1909	3,015
1910–1919	498
1920–1929	325
1930–1939	24
1940–1949	54
1950–1959	746

(Martin A. Bierbaum, "Hoboken, A Come-Back City: A Study of Urban Revitalization in the 1970s," PhD diss., Rutgers University, New Brunswick, New Jersey, 1980, p. 75, citing the U.S. Census, 1970)

Yet "Petty commerce was most characteristic of the Italians: the typical Italian businessman was the grocer-saloonkeeper who was also a steamship ticket agent, labor agent, private banker, and notary public."[168]

Saloonkeeping, like grocery store ownership, was a relatively easy way for an immigrant to gain a foothold in his new home. In many instances, the family lived above or behind the bar or store and wives and children were used as cooks, waiters and bartenders. Reflecting the smallness of the Italian

Captain Berckmann's Café, 200 Bloomfield Street. *Hoboken Historical Museum.*

community in the 1880s, Hoboken had only two Italian saloonkeepers in 1885: Anthony Garibaldi and J. and A. Podesta and Company. Anthony Garibaldi owned a saloon at 149 First Street in 1885, and a year later he and his brother, Louis, opened another saloon next door at 147 First Street. The Garibaldis lived on Adams Street, first at 57 Adams and then at 75 Adams, in the heart of Hoboken's Italian neighborhood. By 1894, the Garibaldi brothers owned two saloons, one at 415 First Street and the other at 301 Grand Street. The wine and liquor merchant John Podesta lived at 332 Adams Street but had his business at 154 Washington Street.[169]

By 1894, out of 240 saloon owners in Hoboken, 14—Andrew Boccoli at 500 First Street, the Garibaldi brothers at 415 First and 301 Grand Street, Aniello Lanzetta at 550 Fifth Street, John B. Lavezo at 551 First Street, Joseppe Luciano at 201 Grand Street, John Marcenaro at Third and Park Avenue, C. Marrone at 600 Adams Street, Anthony Monaco at 332 Madison and 634 Grand Street, John Peluso at 531 Adams Street, Anthony Raffo at 633 Willow Avenue, John Raffo at 210 First Street, John Richetto at 78

Jefferson Street and John Zuvella at 311 Adams Street—had Italian-sounding names. Nearly all of these saloons were located in the Third Ward.[170]

In 1905, Hoboken had 281 saloons, but only thirty-two bar keepers had Italian-sounding names.[171] In 1915, the city had 332 saloons, with about 80 being owned by Italians. The Garibaldis were still in business thirty years later at the same addresses, as was Cesearo Marrone, still at 600 Adams Street. Antonio Raffo was also still in business but now at 98 Garden Street. John Podesta and his partner, most likely his brother, Angelo, had split up at the turn of the century and now operated different establishments, Angelo at 832 Washington Street (in 1905) and 834 Washington Street (in 1915) and John at 100 Bloomfield Street and 350 First Street (in 1905) and then at 350 First Street and 334 Washington Street (in 1915). John Podesta's four sons—August, John Jr., Victor and Albert—also worked as clerks in the family's wine business, as did Angelo's sons, John and Charles.[172] As with German and Irish immigrants, these Italians found prosperity and respectability in Hoboken's thriving liquor industry.

Virtually all Italian immigrants to the United States, and to Hoboken, were Roman Catholic. In Manhattan, the Irish-dominated church leadership literally exiled Italian immigrants to the basement of New York City's first Italian-built Catholic church, the Church of Our Lady of Mount Carmel at 111th Street in East Harlem, causing the Italians to practice their form of Catholicism through street festivals.[173] In Hoboken, Irish and Italians were most likely to come into contact at St. Joseph's Catholic Church on Monroe Street, but there is no evidence of the same degree of conflict between Irish and Italian Catholics in Hoboken as in New York. Nonetheless, in 1888, Italian parishioners of St. Joseph's petitioned Bishop Wigger to establish an Italian parish in Hoboken. Among their supporters was Father Dominic Marzetti, the Italian priest at St. Joseph's. Since many Italians lived in the neighborhood around Jefferson and Third Streets, it was decided to locate the new church there. In 1889, St. Francis Church was completed, and Father Marzetti became the head priest there until his death in 1902.[174]

The other Italian parish in Hoboken, St. Ann's Church, was established in 1900. Services were first held in a chapel located in a storefront building at the corner of Seventh and Adams Streets owned by the members of the St. Ann's Society. The current St. Ann's Church was built at the corner of Jefferson and Seventh Streets in 1926.[175]

The "New Immigration" to Hoboken

Unlike the Irish or even the Germans, Italians were slow to develop a pan-Italian/Italian American ethnic identity that could help them mobilize and organize the community around various political issues. According to historian Rudolph J. Vecoli:

> *The intense sentiment of campanilismo (parochialism) which dictated that the townsmen cluster together in a particular quarter also caused the immigrants to shun Italians from other villages and provinces…Within the settlement of townsmen the traditional relationships and customs of the paese (town) were perpetuated, and the daily round of activities was restricted in so far as possible among the paesani (townsmen). When numerous enough, each group had its own doctors, groceries, saloons, and even church.*[176]

Mutual aid societies helped reinforce this parochialism, with membership typically being restricted to only those from a particular Italian town or village, and the many short-lived Italian language weekly newspapers also fanned regional and local rivalries. Hoboken's Italian men's social clubs are the descendants of these hometown mutual aid societies.

"The failure of the Italians to rise as a group in power and prestige as rapidly as the Irish or Germans was due in large measure to their lack of unity," according to Vecoli. "The Italians, for example, were singularly unsuccessful in establishing organizations and institutions which would promote the welfare of their ethnic group."[177] He added: "The disunity of the Italians was responsible for their failure to achieve political recognition in New Jersey for almost half a century."[178] It was not until 1947 that Italian Americans gained control of Hoboken's city government with the election of Fred M. De Sapio as mayor and several other Italian Americans as city commissioners.

This parochialism also affected Hoboken's Italian cultural institutions. Different groups of Italians established different religious festivals based on traditions in their home regions. The Feast of the *Madonna Dei Martiri* (Virgin of the Martyrs) originated in Molfetta, while the Feast of St. Ann was founded by immigrants from Monte San Giacomo in Salerno. The St. Ann's festival started when that congregation combined the observation of the Feast of St. Ann's on July 26 with the Feast of San Giacomo (St. James)

The procession of the Madonna during the Feast of St. Ann's, date unknown. *Hoboken Historical Museum.*

on July 25 to celebrate the construction of its first church structure in 1910.[179] The Society Madonna Dei Martiri, which was organized in 1927, used to be based at St. Ann's Parish, but a conflict within the congregation in the late 1940s resulted in the society moving to St. Francis Church, which is also home of the Feast of St. Anthony. These festivals continue to be observed as separate statements of Italian and Italian American identity in Hoboken.[180]

Yet most other Hobokenites viewed Italians as homogeneous and culturally very foreign. There were tensions between Irish Americans and Italian immigrants in particular, as both groups congregated uneasily in the city's Catholic churches and parochial schools. In 1909, for example, Italian hostility toward the predominantly Irish American police force boiled over into a shooting match when officers arrived at the scene of an accidental death of a child on the 400 block of Monroe Street. Luckily, no one was killed, although one man was wounded and several people were arrested.[181]

As Italians carved out their neighborhood in the Third Ward and established businesses and cultural and religious institutions, other immigrant

The Scandinavian Lutheran Church, 833 Clinton Street, circa late 1890s. *Hoboken Historical Museum.*

groups continued to try to find their places in Hoboken's ethnic tableau. For a brief time in the 1890s, Hoboken had a Croatian newspaper, *Napredak* (Progress), published by A.G. Skrivanic beginning in 1891, and a Slavonian Benevolent Society, the *Slavjansko Dobrotvorno Drutvo*, which was organized in 1890.[182] Also during this time, the city's Norwegian community built the Scandinavian Lutheran Church at the corner of Ninth and Clinton Streets in 1893. To keep the costs down, the parishioners, many of whom were skilled craftsmen who donated their labor, built the building without a foundation. There was also a Norwegian Congregational Church, founded in 1890 and located on Willow Avenue near Fifth Street.[183] Hoboken had approximately 154 Norwegians, 185 Swedes and 100 Danes in 1890; whether the Swedes and Danes worshipped at the Norwegian churches or were members of other congregations is not known.[184]

Despite increased Italian and Eastern European migration and settlement in the 1890s and early 1900s, the predominance of German, Irish, British and Scandinavian immigrants in Hoboken continued. The number of

The First Dutch Reformed Church, Hudson Street between Fifth and Sixth Streets, after a fire, February 22, 1891. *Hoboken Historical Museum.*

Russian and Polish-born residents continued to be small, particularly when compared to New York City's burgeoning Slavic population. Holland America's pier ensured that Hoboken would continue to receive Dutch, as well as French and Belgian, immigrants in the early twentieth century.[185]

In 1910, Hoboken achieved its highest level of population: 70,324 persons, a 29.7 percent increase over 1900. The town was virtually all white (Hoboken had only 120 blacks, 2 percent of the population; 42 Chinese and 1 Japanese person). Although native-born whites composed about 60 percent of the population, 45.4 percent of the native-born population were the children of immigrants. Only 13,463 Hoboken residents were native born with native-born parents, just 19 percent of the city's population.[186] Thus, despite more than fifty years of steady immigration and settlement, Hoboken remained a predominantly immigrant city, with immigrant communities receiving constant cultural replenishment from the Old Country.

Although Hoboken continued to be a predominantly German city, in 1910, for the first time, Italians replaced the Irish as the second largest immigrant group in town, with twice as many Italian-born residents as Irish-born. Other sizeable immigrant groups came from Russia, Austria and Norway.[187]

TABLE 11. FOREIGN-BORN BY ORIGIN, 1890–1910

	1890	1900	1910
Total	17,431	21,380	27,668
Germany	9,949	10,843	10,018
Ireland	3,862	3,807	3,077
Italy	790	2,360	6,555
Other Europe			
England	915	929	934
Scotland	370	895	338
Wales	17	12	N/A
Austria	150	463	1,368
Holland	58	139	410
Belgium	49	88	230
Luxembourg	1	1	N/A
Switzerland	184	150	221
Norway	154	437	1,047
Sweden	185	330	393
Denmark	109	200	266
Finland	N/A	22	N/A
Russia	54	432	1,639
Hungary	14	62	521
Bohemia	4	8	N/A
Poland	20	103	N/A
France	161	131	107
Spain	8	8	N/A
Portugal	1	1	N/A
Greece	4	17	N/A

	1890	**1900**	**1910**
Americas			
Canada and Newfoundland	191	199	137
Canada (French)	N/A	34	N/A
Cuba and West Indies	36	35	N/A
Mexico	8	5	N/A
Central America	1	25	N/A
South America	17	11	N/A
Asia			
China	26	61	42
Japan	0	2	N/A
India	0	3	N/A
Other	N/A	2	N/A
Africa	11	7	N/A
Australia	8	3	N/A
Other	74	55	N/A

(U.S. Census)

Where these immigrants and their children lived in Hoboken varied considerably. Although Germans lived in every ward, twice as many lived in the First Ward as in any other neighborhood. Their German-speaking brethren, the Austrians, clustered in the Third and Fourth Wards, with few living in the heavily German First Ward. The Irish, meanwhile, continued to concentrate in the Third Ward, with large numbers also living in the Fourth and Fifth Wards. The Third Ward was also becoming heavily Italian, with large numbers of Italians also living in the Fourth Ward. The Norwegians were found primarily in the Fifth Ward, while the Russians based their community in the Fourth Ward.[188] Thus, while some groups predominated in certain neighborhoods, no immigrant group lived exclusively in one area or even had more than a majority in a ward.

TABLE 12. HOBOKEN POPULATION BY WARD, RACE, AND NATIONALITY, 1900

POPULATION	TOTAL	WARD 1	WARD 2	WARD 3	WARD 4	WARD 5
1900	59,364	10,955	8,472	14,218	14,983	10,736
Ethnicity:						
White	59,200	10,933	8,437	14,203	14,905	10,722
Negro	101	2	22	8	62	7
Chinese	61	20	13	7	16	5
Japanese	2	0	0	0	0	2
Origin:						
Native	37,984	6,139	5,734	8,498	9,777	7,836
Foreign	21,880	4,816	2,738	5,720	5,206	2,900

(U.S. Census, 1900)

TABLE 13. HOBOKEN POPULATION BY WARD, RACE, AND NATIONALITY, 1910

POPULATION	TOTAL	WARD 1	WARD 2	WARD 3	WARD 4	WARD 5
1910	70,324	11,657	10,145	19,207	15,802	13,513
Ethnicity:						
Native white/native parents	13,463	1,826	2,664	2,201	3,100	3,672
Native white/foreign or mixed parents	29,030	4,332	3,892	8,369	6,597	5,850
Foreign-born white	27,668	5,456	3,569	8,627	6,032	3,984
Negro	120	42	8	5	63	2

POPULATION	TOTAL	WARD 1	WARD 2	WARD 3	WARD 4	WARD 5
Chinese & Japanese	43	11	12	5	10	5
Foreign-born origin:						
Austria	1,368	221	130	511	438	68
Belgium	230	37	23	90	68	12
Denmark	266	54	98	41	16	57
England	934	125	228	220	138	223
Germany	10,018	3,162	1,854	1,787	1,749	1,466
Holland	410	98	107	124	30	51
Hungary	521	141	75	76	166	63
Ireland	3,077	564	326	801	691	695
Italy	6,555	450	92	4,157	1,441	415
Norway	1,047	90	174	243	61	479
Russia	1,639	224	110	287	927	91
Scotland	338	27	77	62	31	141
Sweden	393	87	78	61	75	92
Switzerland	221	50	41	49	39	42
Other countries	651	126	156	118	162	89

(U.S. Census, 1910)

Despite their growing numbers, Italians, Slavs and other recent immigrant groups were largely shut out of local politics. This was due to the fact that few had been in the United States long enough to have naturalized, and many recent immigrant men did not intend to settle permanently in America but hoped to earn enough money to improve their lives in Europe. Like many cities with large immigrant populations, Hoboken had a low naturalization rate. Only 5,796 immigrant men were naturalized out of a total eligible population of 13,562 foreign-born white males in 1910.[189]

Also, more established groups, such as the Irish, Germans and English, had greater experience with the American political system and, increasingly, vested political interests to defend. Aliens who naturalized and their American-born adult children could, of course, vote, but political power in Hoboken (and Hudson County) continued to be held by Irish Americans, who had, after all, been in the city since the 1840s. As Hoboken's Irish community found itself increasingly outnumbered, both in absolute numbers and percentage of population in the 1910s, its American-born political leaders concentrated their hold on local political power.

Since incorporation in 1855, Hoboken had a mayor and a board of common council, with each of the wards having two representatives who served staggered two-year terms. The mayor also served a two-year term. The Hoboken mayor was a strong position; the mayor could veto all legislation and was an ex-officio member of nearly all of the city's boards: health, police and education (but not fire). The mayor was also the president of the police board and appointed the trustees of the Free Public Library and the commissioners of taxes. The mayor and the council together had the power to issue bonds or other forms of debt and to appoint members to the city's boards.[190] Clearly, the mayoral position was a desirable one to have, and between 1855 and 1915, most of Hoboken's mayors were Anglo-Americans or German Americans.

But as Hoboken grew in population and the number of structures crowded into the mile-square boundaries, the city's business community grew frustrated with the common council's resistance to what businessmen saw as necessary development to improve life and commerce in the city. Businessmen influenced by the Progressive movement also sought greater efficiency and rationality in city government, which they believed the more democratic ward system prevented. And many middle-class Hobokenites, regardless of ethnicity, were unhappy with the influence that working-class Irish American politicians had over city politics.

In 1911, Hoboken's prosperous German American and Anglo-American residents joined forces to challenge Hoboken's "boss," Patrick R. "Paddy" Griffin. An Irish immigrant who had moved first to Brooklyn before settling in Hoboken, Griffin got his political start working as a bartender in the Fourth Ward and then at another Irish saloon in the First Ward. Griffin served as a ward heeler for fellow Irish American politicians Jack Haggerty and Maurice

GUSTAV BACH
DIRECTOR OF
REVENUE & FINANCE

JAMES H. LONDRIGAN
DIRECTOR OF STREETS
& PUBLIC IMPROVEMENTS

BERNARD N. MCFEELY
DIRECTOR
OF PUBLIC SAFETY

HARRY L. SCHMULLING
DIRECTOR OF PARKS
& PUBLIC PROPERTY

PATRICK
R. GRIFFIN
MAYOR
DIRECTOR OF
PUBLIC
AFFAIRS

1918

BOARD OF COMMISSIONERS
CITY OF HOBOKEN.

The Hoboken Board of Commissioners, circa 1918–20. *Hoboken Historical Museum.*

Stack, becoming assistant city clerk in 1904. In 1908, Griffin toppled Stack and took over the city's Democratic organization. He served as a common council member and then as mayor from 1915 until 1926, when he was forced into retirement due to alleged mental instability (Griffin's family and his lieutenants became concerned about his penchant for distributing large sums of money to shoeshine boys and other low-level service workers).[191]

The sources of Griffin's power were his organizational skills and his ability to mobilize Hoboken's large Irish American community to vote as Griffin directed. To get supporters to the polls, Griffin oversaw a forty-five-man committee, with each member representing part of a city ward. Each committee member was responsible for guaranteeing that a certain number of Democratic votes were cast in his neighborhood. In the tradition of nineteenth-century and early twentieth-century machine politics, the local Democratic Party was not particularly scrupulous about how its vote quotas were obtained, and vote buying, ballot stuffing and police pressure were common. Bribery of independent candidates and council members also undermined anti-machine campaigns.

The progressives attempted to strike at Griffin's power by changing the type of government the city had from a mayor and a city council to a commission form of government, which combined the executive and legislative functions of municipal government (the mayor was chosen from among the five commissioners). Each commissioner was responsible for a particular function, such as sanitation or police, theoretically making city performance more transparent and the commissioners more accountable to voters. The commission system of government also replaced the system of ward-based elections every two years with a commission of five members who were elected citywide to four-year terms. Such a form of municipal government was authorized in New Jersey by the Walsh Act of 1911.

The chief motivation for progressives' wanting to change the council system was that while the mayor had often sided with the business community on development issues, council members representing the working-class districts in the western part of town had frequently blocked capital improvement proposals, particularly ones to improve the drainage of the meadow lowlands west of Willow Avenue and upgrade the city's increasingly antiquated sewage system. Middle-class activists alleged also that these council members had given sewer and road contracts to supporters of the local Democratic machine, who in turn paid kickbacks and other campaign contributions to Griffin.[192]

The accusations of political corruption had an undercurrent of ethnic rivalry. The Democratic Party in Hudson County was dominated by Irish immigrants and Irish Americans; Griffin was born in Ireland, and his lieutenants—Bernard "Barney" McFeely, a Fourth Ward trash hauler, and James H. Londrigan, a shirt cutter from the Third Ward—were the sons of Irish immigrants. The only prominent non-Irish member of Griffin's machine was German American Gustav Bach, a bartender who was elected to the council in 1902. Germans in Hoboken tended to vote Republican, but not always, and as usual, the German community was divided by socioeconomic class and religion.[193]

Griffin played a combative form of politics, reflecting both ethnic and class identities. Initially, the Democrats opposed the Walsh Act and the commission form of government. Griffin attacked progressive leader and German American businessman William Keuffel (of the instrument-manufacturing business Keuffel and Esser) and his fellow businessmen as "silk stockings" who would oppress the voters as they oppressed their workers. Griffin consistently connected reformers to the city's big businesses, emphasizing the progressives' elite backgrounds. Although Hoboken voters approved the commission form of government, the measure won by only three votes, and by the time of the election of the new commissioners, March 16, 1915, Griffin and the Democrats had organized a strong slate to challenge the disorganized progressive and Republican candidates. It did not help the reformers that fifty-one candidates competed for five seats.

Although the progressives were successful in getting Hoboken to adopt the commission form of government in 1915, they failed miserably in trying to dislodge Griffin. Griffin organized a successful slate and gained control of the new commission, getting himself elected as a commissioner and then having himself appointed as mayor.[194] Griffin lieutenant Bernard McFeely, who had already served multiple terms as city councilman from 1906 to 1914, was elected commissioner of public safety, which gave him control of the lucrative patronage jobs in the police and fire departments. Gustav Bach was also elected to the new commission and became water commissioner.

Although the working-class residents of the Third and Fourth Wards were successful in defeating efforts by uptown residents to improve the sewer system, they had to live with the consequences: regularly flooded streets, basements and businesses; respiratory diseases caused by mold and greater humidity; and waterborne diseases spread by contaminated water. And although Irish Americans could derive ethnic and religious pride from the predominance of Irish names among city leaders, they also had to pay the "machine tax," monthly contributions to the local Democratic Party. Those who did not had a harder time finding work, could not get the necessary permits to run their businesses or were inexplicably cut off from city charity.

Italian, Russian, Norwegian and other immigrant groups settling in Hoboken in the early 1900s struggled to carve out political, economic and cultural opportunities for themselves in a town dominated by Germans and Irish. In 1917, the institutional structure of Hoboken's German community would be destroyed by the nationalism and xenophobia triggered by World War I. Germans and German Americans continued to live in Hoboken in large numbers, but after 1917, Hoboken would no longer be "Little Bremen."

6

HEAVEN, HELL OR HOBOKEN,
1917–1919

The United States entered World War I on the side of Great Britain, France and their allies on April 6, 1917, and Hoboken residents felt the consequences of war immediately. Who suffered and who prospered in Hoboken during World War I depended almost entirely on national origin or descent. Hoboken's German residents were the main losers. Declared "enemy aliens" by the federal government, many Germans were detained, arrested and evicted from their homes; businesses and jobs were lost; and the institutional structure of the community was dismantled within nineteen short and painful months. Irish and Irish American residents, despite their antipathy for Great Britain, at least did not speak the now-hated German language and were able to maintain their control of city government. Italian-born Hobokenites benefited from the fact that their homeland was one of the United States' allies, and some were able to secure jobs or take over businesses from Germans who ultimately left the city. And Americans of British descent were finally able to counter Germans' confident arrogance and pluralistic vision of America by defining English as the "American" language and Anglo-American culture as American culture.

Hoboken played a central role in President Woodrow Wilson's war policy, and the federal government gave with one hand and took away with the other. Hoboken was declared the main point of embarkation for the U.S. Expeditionary Force (as the U.S. Army sent to Europe was called), and some local businesses—particularly the Remington Arms Company—received major munitions contracts and provided thousands of jobs. American Lead Pencil Company was another recipient of government largess (war expands government bureaucracy, and bureaucrats use a lot of pencils), as was the dry dock company Tietjen and Lang.[195] According to one scholar, during the war "Hoboken prospered. Its restaurants and saloons were crowded, its hotels jammed beyond capacity. Employment was high, and the waterfront reverberated twenty-four hours a day."[196]

But the city coffers and many residents suffered. Immediately after war was declared, the U.S. Army seized the piers and ships owned by Hamburg-America and North German Lloyd, closed most of the city's saloons and forced the firing of hundreds of German and German American workers. The nationalization of the German shipping lines' property and the closure of hundreds of businesses eliminated major sources of revenue for the city. The seizure of the piers alone resulted in the city losing more than 15 percent of its assessable realty, an annual sum of $312,775. The closure of the saloons cost the city government another $200,000 per year in liquor licenses, not including the taxes assessed on the property where the taverns stood. Although the high war industries employment provided some economic stimulus, many Hobokenites lost their jobs, and the city experienced an overall economic decline as a result of the war.[197] World War I thus permanently changed the political, economic and cultural dynamics of Hoboken and had far-reaching social and economic effects on the city.

As a port city, Hoboken felt the effects of the war long before the United States entered the conflict. The combination of the British blockade of Germany and Germany's use of the U-boat devastated Atlantic shipping and travel. In 1906, the Hamburg-America line had sailed to and from Hoboken 235 times; the other shipping companies might not have sailed as frequently, but there was always a ship arriving at, and another departing from, the Hoboken piers.[198] After war began in Europe in August 1914, such busy transatlantic travel abruptly ended, as warring nations tightened borders and would-be immigrants were unable to leave Europe (1,218,480 immigrants entered the United States in 1914; only 326,700 did so in 1915). Between August 1914 and April 1917, only one ship docked at Hoboken, and the Port of New York was crowded with twenty-seven German ships unable to leave the still-neutral harbor. Waterfront jobs were lost as longshore work dried up, and sailor's bars and boardinghouses began to suffer from the loss of business.[199]

There was a brief surge in traffic in the fall of 1914 as immigrant men returned to Europe to fight in their homelands' armies, but then the piers became disturbingly quiet. In November 1916, the Hamburg-America luxury liner, the *Vaterland*, hosted a huge charity ball to raise money for the war charities of the Central Powers. The lavish event was attended by such notables as William Randolph Hearst, Metropolitan Opera tenor Jacques Urlus and 650 other elite members of New York's German American community.[200] Then, on April 6, 1917, after several weeks of increasing tension following Germany's resumption of submarine warfare, the United States declared war on Germany.[201]

With the declaration of war, the United States set into motion its tentative plans for mobilization. Two policies in particular had significant and long-lasting effects on Hoboken: the internment of "enemy aliens" (citizens of countries now at war with the United States) and the seizure of ships and other property belonging to German companies.

The long buildup to war in the winter of 1916–17 gave the federal government time to prepare lists of German and Austro-Hungarian citizens it considered potential threats to the war effort. On the day that war was declared, Friday, April 6, thirteen prominent Germans, including the Reverend Dr. Herman Bruckner of St. Matthew's German Lutheran Church, were arrested in New York and New Jersey by Department of Justice agents.[202]

The forty-four-year-old Bruckner was arrested at his home at 57 Eighth Street while five hundred members of his congregation were at the church waiting for him to preside over a Good Friday service. Many of the Germans arrested and detained at Ellis Island were prominent businessmen who worked for German banks, the shipping lines and chemical and radio transmission companies. Bruckner seems to have been targeted because he was the president of the German Seaman's House in Hoboken and, it was alleged, had acted as an intermediary for imprisoned German sailors in Jamaica (then an English colony), transmitting their mail and sending them such supplies as cigarettes. Bruckner had also drawn attention to himself in 1915, when he had sworn an affidavit to the German ambassador Johann von Bernstorff that he had seen guns on the Cunard ship *Lusitania* before it sailed on its ill-fated voyage to Great Britain.[203] After extensive lobbying and the posting of a $500 bond, Bruckner was finally released from Ellis Island in late August 1917.[204]

The employees of the German shipping lines were also arrested and detained at Ellis Island, not only because they were aliens, but also because they worked for foreign corporations vital to the German war effort. The head of security for the Hamburg-America line, Paul Koenig; pier superintendents Captain Otto Wolpert and Captain Eno Bode; and fellow employee Henry von Staden were among those arrested in the first days of the war. Others, such as North German Lloyd superintendent Max Muller and his son-in-law, Fred Jarka, who worked for Hamburg-America, were simply evicted from their waterfront homes.[205]

Several of these men had been involved in suspicious activity in 1914–17. Koenig had been arrested in 1916 for conspiring to blow up the Welland Canal that connected Lake Ontario and Lake Erie. He had pled guilty in June 1916 to trying to buy information about Allied arms shipments but was released on his own recognizance until his trial, not yet underway in April 1917. Wolpert was under indictment for allegedly plotting to smuggle bombs onto Allied ships.[206] Another German citizen, Fritz Kolb, had been arrested in his room in the Commercial Hotel at 212 River Street in March and a month later was convicted and sentenced to a maximum of five years in state prison for possessing explosives.[207] In the first few months of the war, other Germans in Hoboken were arrested for alleged espionage and bomb making.[208]

The U.S. government had grounds to be suspicious of German citizens in Hoboken. Ever since the mysterious destruction of a munitions dump at Black Tom Island off the shore of Jersey City on July 30, 1916—an explosion that had shattered glass as far away as Times Square and had (amazingly) only killed five—people had been nervous about the growing number of unexplained fires and explosions in the New York City area.[209] Hoboken's reputation as "Little Bremen," and the location and importance of the German shipping companies to Hoboken, caused many Americans both in and outside of government to suspect German Hobokenites of being less than 100 percent loyal to the United States. The large size of Hoboken's German community also allowed German agents and others loyal to the German Imperial government to easily blend into the local German population. Although Hoboken Deutscher Club president August

Vintschger declared that the city's Germans were loyal Americans, the arrests and detentions of enemy aliens continued unabated.[210]

But it was the seizure of the German shipping lines' piers and liners and the subsequent militarization of the waterfront that affected far more Germans and German Americans than did the internment of a few prominent Germans.

The Wilson administration's policy toward German property in the United States developed in fits and starts over the course of several months, and questions of property rights, ownership and compensation were not resolved until the summer of 1918. Using the argument that certain property, especially ships and piers, were vital to the German war effort and therefore forfeit, the United States confiscated several million dollars' worth of German property in the first weeks of war.

In Hoboken, the confiscation began the same day war was declared. At dawn on April 6, 1917, three hundred customs officials and soldiers from the Twenty-second U.S. Infantry seized twenty-seven German ships in the Port of New York, several of them docked at the Hoboken piers. Approximately

German ships at Hoboken, originally published on March 30, 1916, by the Bain News Service. *Library of Congress.*

eleven hundred German crew members, as well as officers' families and women and children from the German colony of Tsing-Tao, China, had been living on board the ships since the outbreak of the war in August 1914. Now they were to be interned on Ellis Island for the duration of the war. A large crowd of Hoboken residents gathered to watch the sunrise operation, which had been anticipated by the German crews since the United States broke off diplomatic relations with Germany in early February 1917. Reflecting the longtime relationship between port authorities and the German captains, port collector Dudley Field Malone hosted the officers from the Hamburg-America ships to breakfast at the Duke's House hotel while the North German Lloyd officers and other port officials ate at the Hof Brau Haus before the Germans were taken to Ellis Island.[211]

Two weeks later, the federal government seized the piers belonging to the Hamburg-America and North German Lloyd lines, bringing three companies of soldiers over from New York in the middle of the night on April 19 to take control of the facilities.[212] Army officials delighted in their stealthy takeover of the German piers:

> *Along River street, where the old Bock beer signs of the German occupation still marked the Deutsche Gartens and Kursaals, tramped the men of San Antonio and the Rio Grande. Fat German saloonkeepers and the fraus and frauleins looked askance at this new invasion. Their Kaiser had said that America would never enter the war—that troops would never sail the seas; and now, only a few weeks after our declaration of hostilities, an army was in motion. Something was wrong in the firm of "Me and Gott." At first the men were held in their troop trains at the Jersey City yards, but they were soon brought into town. So silently and so efficiently was the work done that few of the millions across the water knew that the eastward tide of American soldiers had begun.*[213]

By the end of the day, the dozens of beer kegs that the shipping companies had been storing for reshipment to Germany had been carted away, pup tents had been put up in the yards of the piers and moving vans had arrived to pack up the German pier superintendents' things and convert their homes into officers' quarters. To try to eliminate the dominance that the German companies had once had on the Hoboken waterfront, the United States government renamed the Hamburg-America line's piers from Numbers 1, 2 and 3 to Numbers 4, 5 and 6, while the North German Lloyd line's three piers were renamed Numbers 1, 2 and 3, thus confusing an entire generation of Hobokenites.[214]

The United States had two goals in seizing the German ships: first, it intended to keep them out of its new enemy's hands, and second, the Americans hoped to convert the large luxury liners into troop transport ships. But the German crews had disabled their vessels' engines; only the massive *Vaterland*, owned by Hamburg-America, was not damaged.[215] (On August 31, 1918, a record 46,214 soldiers shipped out of the Port of New York; the *Vaterland*, renamed *Leviathan*, alone carried 12,000 men.)[216] Ultimately, the United States salvaged twenty German liners and converted them into troop transports, and these ships, along with twenty-three others, made 936 transatlantic sailings to transport the American army and its war materiel to Europe.[217]

Although the military took over the piers in April 1917, it was not until the end of June 1918 that the federal government made the confiscation official. In late March 1918, the U.S. Senate voted unanimously, with little debate, to authorize the president to seize and sell the German piers under the Trading with the Enemy Act. The Senate also voted to authorize the president to seize and sell all German-owned or controlled property in the country to "extinguish every vestige of Junkerism from America forever."[218]

Ultimately, the federal government centralized its control over the Port of New York and other ports by placing all harbor work under the management of the Department of Labor's Employment Service in June 1918. The Port of New York employed forty thousand stevedores and longshoremen working on nearly 750 miles of waterfront.[219]

With the army camping out on the German piers and the decision to make Hoboken the Port of Embarkation for the American Expeditionary Force, the city acquired a new, militaristic atmosphere. Life for Hoboken's large German community immediately became very difficult. Citizens of Germany, Austria-Hungary and the Ottoman Empire were required to register with the government as enemy aliens, and President Wilson had proclaimed that no enemy aliens would be allowed to live within a half mile of facilities to be used in the war effort. Although military authorities reassured residents that they would make an exception in the case of the Mile Square City, German Hobokenites were increasingly nervous.

Then, in late May 1917, the Justice Department declared that all the piers in the Port of New York were within a "barred zone" in which no enemy alien could live or work without a special permit; twenty thousand German New Yorkers applied for permits on the first day alone.[220]

The combination of not being allowed on the waterfront and discrimination resulted in thousands of Germans losing their jobs. In Hoboken, two hundred German dockworkers were promptly fired. Another two hundred naturalized United States citizens of German birth who worked on the piers were dismissed by the army quartermaster's department. Their positions were filled by Italians and Italian Americans. The Fletcher Ironworks at Hudson and Fourteenth Streets fired most of its German workers, as did the Pennsylvania Ironworks on River Street, which, as the *New York Times* commented, "took the precaution several weeks ago to get rid of all German, Austrian, and Hungarian help and employ only American or natives of the allied nations."[221] Thousands of teamsters, longshoremen, stevedores and other dockworkers who were either German citizens or German by birth but naturalized U.S. citizens had to find new jobs away from the waterfront.[222] The Griffin administration was quick to take advantage of the situation, and by June, Germans in Hoboken were complaining of having to pay one dollar in graft each day to get the necessary permits to work in the barred zones.[223]

As the army's Port of Embarkation, Hoboken quickly took on the atmosphere of a military town. An estimated 2 million American servicemen passed through Hoboken on their way to Europe between the spring of 1917 and the fall of 1918, although the largest numbers shipped out to Europe in the spring and summer of 1918 after the United States achieved full mobilization.[224] The United States drafted more than 4.7 million men in 1917–18, but only 1.7 million went to Europe, and many never reached the trenches.[225]

Another twenty-four hundred officers and twenty-four thousand enlisted men served in the Embarkation Service, many of them based in Hoboken.[226] These officers lived in rented quarters all over town, despite the challenge of finding rooms in a community infected with, as the *New York Times* described it, "Kaiserliche Teutonicus sympatheticus."[227] The German Sailors Home at 60 Hudson Street was converted into sailors' barracks, and the Grand Hotel Hoboken was taken over by the New York War Camp Community Service and quickly filled to capacity with officers and their families.

Panoramic view of Camp Merritt, New Jersey, U.S. Army cantonment, 1919. *Library of Congress.*

Once officially at war, the federal government activated its selective service system. June 5, 1917, was Registration Day, when all men between the ages of twenty-one and thirty had to register for the military draft, which began on July 20. Each local draft board had a quota; aliens and men with dependents were exempt from service but still had to register. In Hoboken, the draft boards were staffed by Irish American city officials, who drafted Italians in disproportionate numbers. Italians made up 19 percent of the 2,469 Hobokenites inducted but were only 10 percent of the city's population. In June 1918, a new registration for men who had turned twenty-one since May 1917 was created, and in August 1918, Congress extended the eligibility age to between eighteen and forty-five and required a massive new registration.

Most New Jersey men served in the Seventy-eighth and Twenty-ninth Divisions, which included the New Jersey National Guard. After training at hastily built army bases, the draftees went to Camp Merritt, twenty miles north of Hoboken, where they underwent final inspections (especially for influenza and venereal disease), got new uniforms (if needed) and were issued steel helmets and gas masks.

The phrase "Heaven, Hell or Hoboken" began to be heard frequently among the thousands of soldiers arriving from boot camps as they prepared to board ships for Europe. The saying, attributed to American Expeditionary Forces (AEF) commander general John J. "Black Jack" Pershing, was from a comment the general made that the AEF would be in "Heaven, Hell or Hoboken by Christmas" 1917. Unfortunately for the AEF, the war was to last nineteen months.

To assist the military, numerous social service organizations, such as the Young Man's Christian Association, the Red Cross, the Salvation Army, the Knights of Columbus and the Jewish Welfare Board, provided food, entertainment, recreation and spiritual comfort to the soldiers transiting through Hoboken. The "Y" hut in Hudson Square Park was the largest in the country.[228]

In order to be at the Hoboken piers at 8 a.m., the men had to get up about midnight, eat breakfast, and march to the trains or ferries that would take them to their ships. On the pier a long line of soldiers with full packs moved steadily, more or less, to the checkout desk at the foot of the gangplank. There was time for coffee and rolls or ice cream and milk which the Red Cross women provided and a few moments to fill out a safe arrival card which the army would mail when the ship reached its destination. Then they boarded the ship and went below decks where they stayed until the transport cleared the harbor. In the summer of 1918 the army abandoned this needless security measure and permitted the men to come on deck for a last look at the USA.[229]

A new army policy accompanying the pier seizure was that alcohol could not be served within a half mile of an army encampment. Although Hoboken was not technically an army base, the military declared a "saloon curfew," in which waterfront bar owners were informed that they would be shut down if they sold liquor to the soldiers, and last call was established at 10:00 p.m., when reveille was called.[230] Since Hoboken had 326 saloons, many of them located near the waterfront, a confrontation was inevitable. Hoboken saloonkeepers, who had long operated twenty-four-hour establishments, closing only on Sundays (and some not even then), ignored the order and began doing a brisk trade amongst the growing number of soldiers in town.[231]

By early July 1917, the city was in the midst of a full-fledged fight with the army and the federal government to keep open Hoboken's waterfront saloons. General J. Franklin Bell, commander of the Department of the East, declared that all saloons located near the army-occupied piers must close at 10:00 p.m. and stay closed until morning. Of the sixty-one saloons on River and Hudson Streets between Newark and Fourth Streets affected by the new order, fifty-nine were owned by Germans. The military issued the additional threat that any violation of the order by one business would result in the closure of all alcohol-serving establishments within the new military zone.[232]

Although the city's saloonkeepers claimed they would comply with the army's demands, the foot dragging began immediately. Mayor Griffin informed the tavern owners of Bell's new orders on July 3, but a day later it was business as usual on River Street, with saloonkeepers saying that they would remain open past 10:00 p.m. only after they had received official notification from the army. Then they successfully pressured Griffin to lobby the federal government to lessen the hardship the army's presence was inflicting on the city. Colonel J.M. Carsons of the Quartermaster Corps responded with the threat to extend the military zone to a half mile beyond the German piers, which would encompass more than 200 of Hoboken's 326 bars. As German saloonkeepers hired bands and singers to perform for their customers, Hoboken's police force patrolled the waterfront and refused to enforce the army's 10:00 p.m. closure rule.[233]

The army was not amused by this defiance and ratcheted up its demands, insisting that all Hoboken saloons close between 10:00 p.m. and 6:00 a.m. for the duration of the war, not simply those within the four-block military zone by the German piers. The army informed Griffin and the city commissioners that if the board did not pass an ordinance mandating the early closing hours for saloons, the military would seize the saloons, close them and place the city under martial law. Griffin pleaded with Brigadier General N.N. Wright, who oversaw the Port of Embarkation, to limit the alcohol-free zone to the southern end of River and Hudson Streets but was unsuccessful.[234] The military was particularly annoyed by the fact that all but three of the tavern owners who resisted most strongly to the alcohol ban were either German citizens or naturalized U.S. citizens of German birth.[235]

From the beginning of the bar fight, Griffin and other Irish American city officials attempted to straddle the issue between defending the interests of the city's German community and appearing as loyal Americans who supported the war effort. But with his back against the wall, Griffin finally threw his lot in with the saloonkeepers. On July 11, the city commissioners defied the army and passed an ordinance requiring all saloons in town to be closed between midnight and 6:00 a.m. and requested that Hoboken saloons observe state law requiring Sunday closure. City attorney John J. Fallon declared that military authorities had no jurisdiction over Hoboken's liquor businesses and encouraged the mayor and the commissioners to reject the army's demands for a 10:00 p.m. closure. Christopher Bobbe, president of the Hoboken Innkeepers Association and a naturalized U.S. citizen (born in Liverpool to Bremen-born parents), assured the commissioners that Hoboken's saloonkeepers would obey the midnight closure rule, which they did.[236]

Griffin thus cleverly created a situation in which the army's orders were defied yet the saloons were no longer open twenty-four hours and were closed on Sundays, a situation that appeared reasonable to most Hoboken residents and forced the federal government into the position of appearing unreasonable about the two hours between 10:00 p.m. and midnight.

The mayor also asserted that General Bell did not have jurisdiction over Hoboken, which, once it became the Port of Embarkation, fell under General Wright's domain. Griffin even went so far as to assert that Wright had not ordered the saloons to be closed but had only suggested that if the city did not resolve the problem of waterfront saloons, the army would.[237]

For the rest of the summer of 1917, as newly drafted soldiers and sailors began arriving in Hoboken to sail for Europe, Hoboken city officials and the War Department debated questions of jurisdiction and authority. City officials argued that Hoboken's uniquely small size and proximity to the waterfront made applying the half-mile restrictions on alcohol and enemy aliens unfair; a uniform enforcement of the rules threatened to depopulate much of the city and would close virtually all the saloons in town. The army, for its part, insisted that its rules about alcohol near military bases be observed and was angered by the city's refusal to enforce its orders (and even more outraged by the saloons' uniform observance of the city's new midnight closure ordinance).

But in August, city officials began to get tough with saloonkeepers who continued to sell liquor to soldiers to show that the city could manage its own affairs without army interference or assistance. Although most of the waterfront saloons in the military zone were owned by Germans or German Americans, Griffin did not spare Irish bar owners. The mayor ordered Richard Fickers to close his bar at 212 River Street immediately and gave Fickers one week to clean up another saloon he owned at 314 River Street. Fickers's establishment at 212 River Street was an easy choice for Griffin, since it was in the Commercial Hotel, where several Hoboken Germans had conspired to bomb U.S. military sites in the New York area. Griffin also told Michael Foley, who owned a place at Fourth and Bloomfield Streets, that he had one week to sell his bar before the city closed it. Forty-two saloonkeepers were told to stop selling alcohol to soldiers or face closure by the city.[238]

Griffin and other Democrats in Hoboken hoped that the Wilson administration would grant Hoboken an exemption from the half-mile rule. Wilson had been governor of New Jersey before he was president and was familiar with Hudson County and Griffin's well-oiled Democratic machine. Griffin pointed out to the president that Hoboken was not an official military cantonment; there were few troops stationed there (although literally thousands were arriving and shipping out every day), and most of the people managing the piers were civilians. Most importantly, closing the saloons would irrevocably harm the city's economy and tax coffers.

But Wilson would not budge. Elected to his second term only six months before, he had no interest in compromising his war policies to save Hoboken's machine politicians. In fact, Wilson scored valuable political points by making Hoboken the Port of Embarkation. He could ignore Griffin over the bar fight without any fear of electoral consequences, force New Jersey's powerful Irish American Democrats to support his Anglophile foreign policy or have their patriotism questioned and use valuable German property for American military purposes—and do it all in the most German city in New Jersey.

In early October 1917, Hoboken was declared officially dry as the president's proclamation forbidding the sale of alcohol within a half mile of piers under federal control or of munitions plants engaged in government work was enforced. By early November, 168 saloons between Ferry Street (now Observer Highway) and Eighth Street and the waterfront to Jefferson Street had been closed. Another 112 saloons around Fifteenth and Sixteenth Streets were closed once the question of whether the northern piers were being used for military purposes was resolved. In early November, the military extended the dry zone to include the Lamport & Holt Steamship Company at Fifteenth Street. With that extension of the dry zone, only 60 saloons in Hoboken were still in business, all of them west of Jefferson Street,

"Food will win the war. You came here seeking freedom, now you must help to preserve it. Wheat is needed for the allies, waste nothing." A propaganda poster from the U.S. Food Administration in Yiddish, the lithograph designed by C.E. Chambers and published by Rusling Wood, New York, 1917. *Library of Congress.*

in the Italian section of town.[239] A few saloons on River Street that were not owned by Germans stayed in business by selling "near beer."

Imposing prohibition on Hoboken was not the only way the army interfered with life in the city. With the declaration of war, the military claimed priority for a wide variety of staples, and Americans were exhorted to conserve food, fuel, clothing, paper and other materials that could be used to make weapons or supply the army. Food shortages were severe in Hoboken in 1917, and the ability to buy sugar became a question of who knew the right person. Former city councilman James Clark, an Irish American longshoreman, and an Italian grocer were arrested and charged with treason for stealing two barrels of sugar worth fifty-four dollars from a Hoboken pier in August 1917.[240] City hall employees were also discovered dealing in sugar ration cards.[241] Germans and others who did not sign pledge cards promising to follow voluntary conservation measures found their names published in the local newspaper as a form of peer pressure.[242]

Although the Hoboken School Board did not immediately jump on the national bandwagon to ban German in the public schools, by the start of the school year in September, it was clear that Hoboken's bilingual English-German educational system would not survive the war. Declaring that there was no longer any advantage to studying German, the school board voted unanimously in September 1917 to drop the teaching of German in the elementary grades and to only allow German as a foreign language to be taught in the high school. Hoboken elementary school German teacher Otto Hoch transformed himself into the high school's "Americanization" teacher, instructing his pupils in U.S. history and citizenship. Much of the opposition to the long practice of requiring German instruction in all the grades came from Italian immigrants, who objected to their children studying the language of a country with which their old and new homes were now at war.[243]

Just as the military was closing Hoboken's saloons, the other shoe dropped for the city's German citizens. On November 16, 1917, President Wilson proclaimed that enemy aliens could not live, work or even travel within one hundred yards of docks, piers and waterfronts. Enemy aliens who lived, worked or owned property within the zone were ordered to move out; about one thousand German families who lived on Hudson Street were evicted. Another eight hundred people were arrested in a series of raids the army conducted on River Street. Anyone who could not prove his citizenship was detained and taken directly to Ellis Island. Mayor Griffin's aide, German-born Albert Struntz, was among the two hundred Germans arrested on November 19 as part of the military's crackdown on enemy aliens living and working near the waterfront. Struntz, who lived at 206 River Street, barely escaped internment when his wife found his citizenship papers and ran them down to the ferry before it sailed for Ellis Island. Besides banning Germans from the new military zone, the permits that had previously allowed Germans to be on the waterfront were revoked, and enemy aliens were not even allowed to ride streetcars or railroads that passed through the zone, even if they were not getting off within the barred area (they were still allowed to ride the ferries). Unlike arrests of Germans in New York in April, the first of these mass raids in Hoboken was conducted by the military without the assistance or even knowledge of the local police.[244]

By mid-February 1918, all male German citizens fourteen years and older were required to register with local police authorities, providing extensive information about their lives and employment histories, as well as photographs and fingerprints. By this point, many Germans had left the city, and so it was estimated that there were only about fifty to sixty German aliens in Hoboken who had refused to register.[245]

The United States achieved full military and economic mobilization in the spring of 1918; more men were drafted in April, May and June 1918 than in all of 1917, and ten thousand men per day were sailing from Hoboken, as well as from Newport News, Virginia; Boston; and Philadelphia. As part of the effort to fight against Germany's Spring Offensive, the U.S. government seized six Dutch ships belonging to the Holland America line in March 1918. The Netherlands, which remained neutral during the war, angered Great Britain and the United States with its continued insistence on the right to trade with Germany, thus breaking Britain's embargo of Germany. The Allies demanded that the Dutch allow Allied armed guards on their ships and the use of Allied crews to man the Dutch ships through the areas of the Atlantic suspected to be patrolled by German submarines. Knowing that the Dutch would refuse such demands, the United States used this pretext to justify its seizure of Dutch shipping property in America. The navy also used the Scandinavian American line's piers in Hoboken.[246]

By this point, the military was fully in charge of most aspects of life in Hoboken. Frustrated with police commissioner Bernard McFeely's lack of

A Liberty Bond ship float at Washington and Sixth Streets, circa June–August 1918. *Hoboken Historical Museum.*

assistance during the bar fight, the army began to "clean up" Hoboken in March, arresting women as prostitutes if they were found walking the streets after dark. "Chop suey" restaurants, as Chinese restaurants were then called, were also ordered to close nightly, causing the late-night establishments, which did most of their business between midnight and 4:00 a.m., to go out of business.[247]

Even those residents who supported the war effort found their daily lives greatly inconvenienced by the military regulations that governed the city. Hobokenites' lack of enthusiasm for the war was expressed in a variety of ways. During the Third Liberty Loan Drive in May 1918, Hoboken residents only bought $3,030,450 worth of bonds out of their quota of $4,194,600, whereas New Yorkers raised more than their quota of $900,000,000—and this despite Mayor Griffin's efforts to stimulate popular support for the loan by climbing to the top of a seventy-five-foot fire ladder and waving an American flag before a crowd of twelve thousand people.[248]

Germans occasionally found ways to subtly resist the war effort. In May 1918, Buffalo head nickels altered to make the Indian's head look like Kaiser Wilhelm were found circulating in Hoboken among newsboys who had received them as payment for newspapers.[249]

More serious was the use of the wartime atmosphere of super-patriotism to pursue personal vendettas or transform personal conflicts into questions of national security, loyalty and patriotism. Neighbors turned on neighbors. German citizen Henry Latrell of 128 Adams Street was badly beaten by his next-door neighbor, Joseph McDonald of 132 Adams Street, for refusing to buy Liberty Bonds in June 1918. Such violence was indirectly encouraged by newspaper headlines, such as the one reporting Latrell's assault: "Enemy Badly Battered, Registered German Alleged to Have Spoken Too Freely."[250] A longshoreman murdered a pressman in a fight, allegedly about the war, in a saloon in July 1918.[251] That same summer, the federal government seized the financial records of the Tietjen and Lang Dry Dock Corporation after secretaries of two draft boards in Hoboken complained that the company was aiding young men in evading the draft by giving them jobs at the dry dock.[252] Germans and German Americans had long dominated Hoboken socially; the city was, after all, known around the world as "Little Bremen." But now, many Hobokenites of British descent saw an opportunity to take the swagger out of the step of the city's German community.

In July 1918, a new round-up of enemy aliens snagged additional German Hobokenites. Ernest Hertel was arrested for expressing the opinion that Kaiser Wilhelm was a better man than President Wilson at a Fourth of July picnic, and two Hoboken women swore out a complaint against a German New Yorker who worked at the Federal Shipping Company in Kearney, New Jersey, for saying that American ships would sink because of faulty riveting work done by German sympathizers at the shipyard.[253]

Hundreds of Hoboken men passively refused to support the war effort by failing to register for the draft, a requirement imposed on all men between the ages of twenty-one and thirty, regardless of citizenship (but only American citizens could be drafted into the service). Once American casualty lists began appearing daily in newspapers in the summer and fall of 1918, Americans became increasingly resentful that non-citizens did not have to serve in the military. In September, the Justice Department, aided by local police and the private American Protective League, launched so-called "slacker raids," in which thousands of young men were accosted at train stations, in theaters and on the street and arrested as "slackers" if they were not able to prove they had registered for conscription. The raids were very heavy handed; in one raid in northern New Jersey, nearly 89,000 men were detained, but only 750 were found to be in arrears with their draft boards. In Hoboken, 2,000 were held in the City Hall Armory, but only 100 of these were deemed "real slackers."[254]

Another hardship that came with the war that fall was the influenza epidemic spread by soldiers traveling to Hoboken on their way to Europe.

"Americans glad to be home—awaiting trains for demobilization camp, Hoboken." A photo stereo card published by Underwood & Underwood, circa 1918–20. *Hoboken Historical Museum.*

The epidemic, which traveled with the troops to Europe and then back to the United States on returning transports, affected one-quarter of the AEF and killed nearly 47,000 soldiers, almost as many as died in combat. Approximately 675,000 Americans died of the flu in 1918–19. Hoboken had seven thousand cases of the flu by early October 1918.[255] Flu victims in Hoboken, both civilian and military, were treated at St. Mary's Hospital, which was taken over by the army and used to treat soldiers too badly injured to be rehabilitated in Europe.

Once fully mobilized for war, the American government had to just as abruptly put on the brakes when the Armistice was declared on November 11, 1918. On that day, several thousand soldiers were on board ships in Hoboken preparing to sail for France.

Although the city's residents celebrated the end of the war, concern about the postwar demobilization quickly emerged. Returning soldiers would need jobs, and lucrative war contracts like those held by the Remington Arms Work, which employed five thousand people making bullet casings, would certainly come to an end.

Initially, Hoboken continued to be a government port. No longer the port of embarkation, it now became the port of debarkation to where the returning American troops sailed, the first arriving on December 2, 1918, on the RSS *Mauretania*. Even more quickly than they had been sent to Europe, the American troops returned home, at a rate of 300,000 per month in the winter of 1918–19.[256]

But Hoboken felt the immediate postwar recession and correspondingly high cost of living sharply, as thousands of workers were laid off and factories readjusted production to peacetime needs. Most importantly, the foundation of the city's economy, the piers, remained in government hands, and when or if they would ever be returned to either private ownership or be given to the city was unknown.

Although the United States' participation in World War I only lasted nineteen months, the war had a profound impact on Hoboken and its immigrant communities. No longer "Little Bremen," Hoboken was a community in flux in the 1920s, and whether it would become a new Molfetta or something else remained to be determined.

ITALIANS VERSUS THE IRISH IN AN ERA OF RESTRICTION, 1920–1950

W orld War I greatly interfered with transatlantic travel and migration. More than 1.2 million immigrants entered the United States in 1914; only 326,700 people came in 1915, a figure that would drop to a low of 110,618 in 1918. Although immigration numbers briefly surged in 1920 and 1921 (to 430,000 and 805,228 entries, respectively) as refugees fled political and economic turmoil in Europe, the United States began restricting immigration in 1921. The decline in the number of immigrants and the corresponding negative impact immigration restriction had on the shipping industry hurt Hoboken economically and socioculturally. Immigration had been good business for Hoboken for nearly one hundred years, but now with the United States establishing quotas of approximately 165,000 people per year, there would be far fewer immigrants passing through and settling in the city in the postwar period.

This change in immigration policy helped transform Hoboken's immigrant communities into ethnic communities based on increasingly distant memories of immigration and life in Europe. The few new immigrants from Germany and Italy who settled in Hoboken in the 1920s and 1930s struggled to fit into existing ethnic communities that split over the question of loyalty to one's ancestral homeland or life in America. Meanwhile, Irish Americans solidified their hold on the city's political life just as Italians were becoming Hoboken's largest ethnic group. But it was not until after World War II that Italian Americans gained the political power that reflected their actual numbers.

After two years of anti-immigrant hysteria during the Big Red Scare of 1919–20, the United States adopted a radical new policy of immigration restriction in 1921. This policy limited immigration to 350,000 entries for 1921–22, with quotas of 3 percent of each nationality living in the United States in 1910. Immigrants from Canada, Mexico and other Western Hemisphere countries and alien children of U.S. citizens were exempt from the quotas. Close relatives of citizens and aliens in the process of naturalizing were given preference in the new quota queue.[257]

The Quota Act went into effect on May 19, 1921, and created immediate chaos in the international migration flow because the United States continued to admit immigrants on a first-come, first-served basis. People in war-torn regions of the world sought to escape to America, arriving only to find that the quota for their particular nation had already been filled and they would not be admitted. Steamship lines raced across the Atlantic in the hopes of getting their passengers to the United States first, despite the fact that only 20 percent of the annual quota for any one nationality was admissible in a given month. A typhus scare in New York City in the spring of 1921 caused further confusion as ships were redirected to Boston and other East Coast ports.[258] In May 1922, the Quota Act was extended for two more years as Congress considered the question of permanent quotas.

In 1924, Congress passed and President Calvin Coolidge signed the Immigration Act of 1924. This legislation tightened the restrictions established in 1921 by reducing the quota percentage from 3 percent to 2 percent and shifting the basis of the quota from the census of 1910 to the census of 1890, when far fewer Eastern and Southern Europeans lived in the United States. Under this new formula, the quota for 1925 and 1926 was 164,667; after 1929, the quota would be reduced to 150,000, with each national quota to be based on "the whole white population of the United States, with due regards to the national origin of that population."[259] For the first time also, would-be immigrants were required to have visas issued by State Department consulates in their home countries, and aliens' identities had to be documented by photographs. Aliens who wanted to leave and then reenter the United States without being subject to the quotas were required to obtain a reentry permit.

Within four years, the United States went from a system of relatively open immigration—in which the burden of proof for exclusion belonged to the federal government, which conducted its inspections at immigration stations such as Ellis Island—to a highly bureaucratic regime in which an alien had to prove his desirability to a consular officer in his home country before being granted a visa that allowed him to enter the United States.

The quotas also ensured that of the few immigrants granted visas, most would be from Northern Europe; the largest quotas went to Germany, Great Britain and Ireland. Italy's quota for 1924–25, for example, was 3,845, while Russia's was just under 2,250. African and Asian countries were granted token quotas of 100 each.[260]

Immigration restriction transformed Hoboken economically and socioculturally. For the first time in the city's history, the continuous cultural replenishment and connection to the "Old Country" were cut off, as immigration was limited by the quotas and then by the Great Depression. Over the course of the 1920s and 1930s, Hoboken's German, Irish, Italian and other immigrant communities primarily comprised American-born children and the grandchildren of immigrants. A Hoboken resident might call him or herself Italian or Irish, but what he or she really was was American of Italian or Irish descent, new ethnic identities that were beginning to transcend old particularistic and local immigrant identities.

Hoboken felt the economic impact of immigration restriction first, as jobs related to the shipping and travel industries dried up. Hoboken had twenty-two hotels in 1915, nearly all of them located on either River or Hudson Streets close to the once-bustling piers. Ten years later, only the Central, the Continental, the Grand, Meyer's and the River View Hotels were still in business.[261] The porters, runners and cabbies who used to cater to immigrant travelers before the war now competed for far fewer customers, many of them now Americans sailing for Europe for business or tourism. Increasingly, the only jobs available on the waterfront were longshore and stevedore jobs.

The City of Hoboken also found itself in difficult financial straits in the early 1920s. The most valuable real estate in town, the German piers, remained in the hands of the War Department, which turned the property over to the U.S. Shipping Board, which in turn leased the piers to various steamship lines.[262] The city's Board of Commissioners objected strongly to the federal government's continued ownership of the piers once the war was over since the city lost thousands of dollars in tax revenues that the German companies used to pay to the city. Before the war, Hoboken's property tax rate was about $22 per $1,000; in 1921, it was more than $42 per $1,000, as the city struggled to fill the large tax hole caused by the war and the nationalization of the piers. By 1920, Hoboken was out more than $525,000, a painful situation made worse by the Griffin administration spending anticipated tax monies that it was unable to collect.[263] In 1921, the federal government paid the city nearly $105,000 in back taxes on the piers previously owned by the North German Lloyd shipping company.[264] And in 1924, the State of New Jersey reimbursed Hoboken for lost tax revenues the city had handed over to the state but had been unable to collect from the federal government or the German companies.[265]

But these sums, as welcome as they were, did not change the fact that the federal government continued to own, and profit off, most of the Hoboken piers.[266] Hoboken's congressman, John J. Eagan, submitted several bills to Congress to gain the city tax relief or, alternately, ownership of the German piers, but these bills went nowhere.[267] The city's inability to control its destiny was highlighted again in 1926, when, despite vocal opposition from the city, the War Department sold the Hoboken Shore Road (also confiscated during the war) to the new Port Authority of New York for $1 million in bonds.[268]

The city was also increasingly frustrated by the federal government's management of the piers. When a spectacular fire on August 24, 1921, badly damaged two of the former Hamburg-America piers, Piers 5 and 6, and threatened the remains of fifteen hundred American servicemen who were stacked on a neighboring pier awaiting return to their loved ones, the federal government was slow to rebuild the facilities, as a private company would have done.[269] From the city's perspective, the government's failure to rebuild the piers—especially Pier 5, which was totally destroyed—was an embarrassment.

Hoboken's declining economic fortunes were reflected in its declining population. The census of 1920 registered the city's first loss in population ever in its history: 68,166 persons in 1920 versus 70,324 residents in 1910. Nearly all of these 2,000 former Hobokenites were German or German American. "Little Bremen" had half the number of Germans it had in 1910. Hoboken also had fewer Austrians, Russians and Irish-born residents.[270]

The decline in the number of Germans in Hoboken corresponded with an increase in the number of Italians; for the first time, Italians were the largest immigrant group in Hoboken, with 7,255 Italian-born residents in 1920, or about 10 percent of the city's population.[271]

TABLE 14. POPULATION OF HOBOKEN IN THE TWENTIETH CENTURY

YEAR	TOTAL POPULATION	FOREIGN BORN	% FOREIGN BORN
1900	59,364	21,380	36
1910	70,324	27,771	39
1920	68,166	23,544	35
1930	59,261	21,193	36
1940	50,115	13,877	28
1950	50,676	*11,238	*22
1960	48,441	22,959	47
1970	45,389	9,193	20

(U.S. Census. *Foreign-born white only).

These immigrants packed into the Third Ward, with more than half of the Italians in the city living in that neighborhood. As Italians moved to the Third Ward, the Irish moved out to the Fifth Ward, which had long been home to many Norwegians. Russians continued to cluster in the Fourth Ward, attracting other Slavic immigrants; half of the city's 210 Czechs, two-thirds of the city's 541 Poles and more than one-third of the 309 Yugoslavs lived in that district.[272] The Germans who remained in town after the war continued to concentrate in the First Ward, which had always been at the heart of the German community in Hoboken.

TABLE 15. HOBOKEN POPULATION BY WARD, RACE, AND NATIONALITY, 1920

POPULATION	TOTAL	WARD 1	WARD 2	WARD 3	WARD 4	WARD 5
1920	68,166	10,691	9,848	18,224	14,050	15,353
Ethnicity:						
Native white/ native parents	14,473	2,225	2,926	2,444	2,677	4,201
Native white/ foreign parents	23,840	3,389	2,681	7,427	5,247	5,096
Native white/ mixed parents	6,105	804	998	1,378	1,169	1,756
Foreign-born white	23,496	4,218	3,231	6,964	4,832	4,251
Negro	204	33	6	7	120	38
Indian, Chinese, Japanese, all others	48	22	6	4	5	11
Foreign-born origin:						
Austria	1,019	211	130	248	264	166
Belgium	310	85	46	89	24	66
Canada	165	16	56	17	20	56
Czechoslovakia	210	43	14	34	101	18
Denmark	309	36	117	30	14	112
England	560	80	145	82	56	197
France	125	32	23	29	22	19
Germany	5,917	1,862	1,316	910	698	1,131
Greece	236	125	33	15	52	11
Hungary	454	77	73	82	132	90
Ireland	2,328	358	338	490	360	782
Italy	7,255	489	148	4,241	1,797	580
Jugo-slavia	309	13	7	121	145	23
Netherlands	767	181	276	130	23	157

Italians Versus the Irish in an Era of Restriction, 1920–1950

Population	Total	Ward 1	Ward 2	Ward 3	Ward 4	Ward 5
Norway	676	88	130	71	34	353
Poland	541	49	16	65	367	44
Russia	1,167	220	143	141	530	133
Scotland	260	41	70	20	33	96
Sweden	276	48	62	36	22	108
Switzerland	144	41	21	29	20	33
Wales	12	0	3	4	1	4
Other countries	456	123	64	80	117	72

(U.S. Census, 1920)

Many of the city's German social clubs, especially the homeland societies, also continued to exist after the war, including the *Turn Verein* (gymnastics club), the *Socialists Männerchor* (men's choir), the Plattdeutsch and Rhinelander Clubs and the Hanover *Frauen Verein* (women's club).[273] And some German immigrants who arrived in the 1920s, such as Henry and Dora Schnackenberg, who opened Schnackenberg's Luncheonette at 1110 Washington Street in 1931, established new businesses and community institutions.[274]

But Hoboken's population continued to decline. In 1930, the city had 59,261 residents, 10,000 fewer than it did in 1920, but this time it was mostly native-born Americans who were leaving in search of new opportunities and a better quality of life. By 1930, two-thirds of the city's population was made up of either immigrants or their American-born children; less than a quarter of Hobokenites had native-born parents. Most of these immigrants and their children were Italian and Italian American.[275]

The departure of so many native-born Americans in the 1920s and 1930s initially caused Hoboken to become more of an immigrant city, but immigration restriction, the lack of economic opportunities during the Depression and World War II prevented other immigrants from rejuvenating the city's immigrant communities as they had in earlier decades. The result was cultural and economic stagnation and entrenchment as the dynamism of the pre–World War I decades dissipated.

TABLE 16. HOBOKEN POPULATION BY WARD, RACE, AND NATIONALITY, 1930

POPULATION	TOTAL	WARD 1	WARD 2	WARD 3	WARD 4	WARD 5
1930	59,261	10,062	10,280	14,530	10,754	13,635
Ethnicity:						
Native white/ native parents	13,372	2,507	3,103	1,807	2,163	3,792
Native white/ foreign or mixed parents	24,221	2,908	3,423	7,547	4,621	5,722
Foreign-born white	21,160	4,601	3,727	5,162	3,597	4,073
Negro	462	27	16	9	367	43
Chinese	33					
Japanese	0					
Mexican	4					
Foreign-born origin:						
Belgium	433					
Czechoslovakia	217					
Denmark	210					
England	499					
France	97					
Germany	5,864					
Ireland	1,425					
Netherlands	809					
Norway	382					
Poland	374					
Scotland	282					
Sweden	182					
Switzerland	82					
Wales	10					
Northern Ireland	159					

Population	Total	Ward 1	Ward 2	Ward 3	Ward 4	Ward 5
Indians	0					
Chinese	33					

(U.S. Census, 1930)

TABLE 17. HOBOKEN POPULATION BY WARD, RACE, AND NATIONALITY, 1940

Population	Total	Ward 1	Ward 2	Ward 3	Ward 4	Ward 5
1940	50,115	6,791	9,154	12,699	8,541	12,930
Ethnicity:						
Native white	35,961	4,311	6,683	9,001	5,943	9,023
Foreign born	13,858	2,375	2,452	3,689	2,458	2,874
Negro	131	80	2	6	138	32
Other races	36	15	15	3	2	1

(U.S. Census, 1940)

Nowhere was this more obvious than in the city's politics. Although Hoboken had fewer and fewer Irish residents, Irish Americans continued to dominate the city's politics, and the political machine of Mayor Patrick Griffin became an extension of Jersey City mayor Frank Hague's Hudson County empire.

As Irish and Irish Americans became ever-smaller minorities in Hudson County, the Hague and Griffin machines consolidated their power over local politics by manipulating elections, rewarding supporters with jobs and other favors and punishing potential opponents. Both Irish Catholic, Hague and Griffin infused their political organizations with an Irish American style of Catholicism: hierarchical, intimate, authoritarian and tolerant of violence.[276] According to historian Bob Leach, "Hagueism was more than a political machine. It was a vast social order, organized upward from the neighborhood level and outward to include all spheres of social activity. It incorporated the schools, the churches, the police, lawyers, doctors, labor unions, and fraternal organizations."[277] Added historian William Lemmey, "Hague made Catholicism the city's quasi-official religion and never separated matters of Church and State."[278]

Under Hague, Jersey City had a particular kind of Irish Catholic morality, one in which prostitution was unacceptable (although not unheard of) but gambling was fine, as long as it was controlled by the machine. Public employees were expected to kick back 3 percent of their salaries each month to the organization and donate their time to get out the vote and supervise the polls on election day. Greater "swag" or riches were found on the piers, where a combination of petty and organized theft by both individual laborers and machine surrogates, as well as the constant threat of machine-orchestrated labor stoppages, were a regular and increasing cost of doing business at the Port of New York.[279]

In Hoboken under Griffin, Catholic morality was laxer, and the Mile Square City became known for prostitution, gambling and, during the 1920s and early 1930s, illegal alcohol. Prohibition was not only not enforced in Hoboken but also barely acknowledged. (The only time bars in Hoboken were closed was during the war when the army enforced prohibition.) Even the local telephone books continued to have numerous "saloon" entries in their business directories. Hoboken had 62 saloons in 1925, a far cry from the 326 saloons in business in 1917 but still a significant number for a city that was supposed to be dry.[280]

As in Jersey City, both public employees and local businessmen were expected to pay a "tax" to the machine for the privilege of operating in Hoboken. Former runner-turned-hotelier Joseph Samperi, who bought the Continental Hotel from its German owners in 1923, was one businessman who ran afoul of the machine for not paying the expected kickbacks on time and in full. His son, Paul Samperi, who was born in 1926, recalled:

> *During Prohibition, raids would be made every so often by federal men, if you were serving liquor. Hoboken was almost an open town. People would come from New York, Weekhawken, all different places, to enjoy themselves in restaurants, speak-easies, nightclubs, taverns, bars. Dad was informed the first time that federal officials were coming over. Usually, when you were informed, you put all your liquor away and you tried to hide everything. You just showed that you were serving near-beer or just soda. But the one time Dad wasn't informed (and I guess McFeely might have been mad at him, because he was the one who would do the informing, he knew who was coming)… They came in, they found liquor behind the bar, and they closed Dad down.*

A month or so later Dad was fined, and also given a prison sentence because it was his second offense. He was sent to Hudson County jail for one month. It was a jail that didn't have any locked doors; you could wear your own suit; you could go out during the day or night if you wanted to, to have dinner out, so long as you were there at night. So it was really a joke, the whole thing.

One time we kind of missed Dad. We didn't know where he was, and Mom said, "We're going to go and see Daddy. He's in Chicago." So we got on the Jackson trolley, went up to Jersey City, made a couple of turns, got off, and there was the Hudson County jail. I think it was my brother who said, "Wow, Mom. Chicago isn't that far away. It's pretty close!" So we went to see Dad and we had a nice afternoon.

But one thing I wanted to mention—Dad could have, if he had wanted to, get a substitute person to go to jail for him for a month. In those days you could do that. But Dad says, "No, I could use the vacation. I'll go to jail, take my penalty." And that was it.[281]

Corruption, always prevalent in local politics, became endemic in Hoboken in this time period. In 1926, public safety commissioner Bernard McFeely replaced Griffin as the Democratic boss of Hudson County, becoming mayor of Hoboken in 1930. Under McFeely's administration, political patronage favoring Irish Americans was perfected to an art. Griffin and other Hoboken machine politicians, such as Thomas J. Kehoe and James F. Londrigan, had appointed family members to city jobs; as commissioner of streets and public improvements, Londrigan, in particular, had been in a key position to dispense patronage because street cleaning was done by hand, using day laborers. But what was distinctive about McFeely was the sheer number of relatives and close friends put on the city payroll. The new mayor appointed his brother, Edward J. McFeely, chief of police; his nephew, Thomas F. McFeely, superintendent of the Hoboken school system; and dozens of other McFeely relatives to various city positions. The McFeely family trash business, which used horse-drawn carts until the late 1940s, always held the city's lucrative garbage hauling contract. And, as commissioner of public safety since 1915, McFeely continued to be responsible for doling out prestigious police and fire jobs.[282] "Appointments to the police and fire departments were not always made with regard to the guidelines set down in municipal statutes, and after such appointments were challenged by the Chamber of Commerce in the courts, Griffin and McFeely simply changed the municipal ordinances to make their appointments legal."[283] By 1950, Hoboken had 1,450 city employees, 875 of them in public administration—a large number for a city shrinking in population.[284]

McFeely's tendency to favor Irish Americans over other ethnic groups in the city angered Italian Americans, who were increasingly conscious of their numerical size and their political marginality. Yet Italian Americans were largely shut out of electoral politics in Hoboken, with a few notable exceptions, the most prominent being Frank Sinatra's mother, Dolly, who was a Democratic Party activist in the Third Ward. "McFeely placed so many family members on the public payroll they alone outnumbered non-Irish officeholders in the Mile Square City. The mayor "hated Italians and did his best to make life miserable for them," according to *Time* magazine."[285]

Largely cut off from public sector jobs, Italians began to seek, and find, work on the piers, a sector of the local economy long dominated by the Irish. Longshoremen on both sides of the Hudson and East Rivers had for some time competed in a vicious struggle for work with other "unskilled" laborers in what was called the "shapeup," the daily hiring of dock workers to load and unload the giant steamships that transported goods around the world.[286] The international economic depression of the 1930s made this competition even fiercer, since fewer manufactured goods and raw materials needed to be loaded up and shipped out from the city's piers. By 1953, when filmmaker Elia Kazan and screenplay writer Bud Schulberg were looking for locations to film *On the Waterfront*, the shapeup and the accompanying corruption were deeply entrenched on both sides of the Hudson River.[287]

According to historian James T. Fisher, despite the geographic closeness and economic interconnectedness of Hoboken and the West Side of New York:

> Hoboken was more ethnically fluid than Chelsea, the West Village, or Hell's Kitchen. Although Italian American longshoremen crammed into their inland enclave "west of Willow" surely did not discern much fluidity in the attitudes of the dominant Irish—from pier hiring bosses to politicians to clerics—the nature of the city's waterfront labor market after 1917 forced interaction between the groups; men scrambled from pier to pier as work became available. Two Italian parishes established by different branches

of the Franciscan Order, St. Francis (1888) and St. Ann's (1900), were well situated to serve the large number of Italian immigrant dockworkers and their families. St. Ann's was especially identified with the preservation of Italian identity and traditions and fostered a strong sense of ethnic solidarity that sustained dockworkers in their struggles with Hoboken's Irish ILA [International Longshoremen's Association] leadership.

On the West Side of Manhattan, Irish American longshoremen might offer financial support to a struggling local Italian parish, but they did not shape up alongside Italians on their piers, as was increasingly the case in Hoboken. That city's Irish and Italians both toiled in the shadow of an imposing German American legacy severed when, in the wake of the First World War, the United States government confiscated the pier sheds of the Hamburg-American and North German Lloyd steamship lines which had towered over the city's waterfront for decades. Their absence left a massive hole in the waterfront economy that was never completely filled, creating a competitive, cost-driven labor market that did not permit the kind of separate Irish labor aristocracies found along Manhattan's West Side, where men worked the piers in long-standing "regular" gangs.[288]

Another factor in Italians' political impotence was the fact that many remained noncitizens, despite the fact that most had immigrated to the United States before World War I. Italians had traditionally had low rates of naturalization, reflecting their relatively short time in the United States, their preference for petty entrepreneurship versus public sector jobs (which were usually reserved for citizens) and their original intention of returning to Italy versus staying permanently in the United States. In 1930, about half of Hoboken's 12,000 foreign-born white men were naturalized, and another 2,250 men had begun the process. Among foreign-born women over twenty-one, the naturalization rate was lower; 4,180 out of 7,700 foreign-born adult women were citizens, and only 530 had taken out first papers to begin the naturalization process.[289]

By 1940, however, the majority of Hoboken's immigrants had assimilated to the degree that they had naturalized, knew how to speak English and spoke their native languages primarily with family and close friends. Although Catholic Church services were still offered in Italian, other denominations held theirs in English, and the Hoboken schools had not been bilingual since 1917. Only about a quarter of the city's foreign-born residents were aliens in 1940, and most had naturalized or were in the process of becoming U.S. citizens.[290]

Immigrants in Hoboken became American citizens for a variety of reasons: restrictive quotas, visas and reentry permits that precluded easy return to the home country and encouraged permanent settlement; citizens' ability to gain close relatives exemption from quotas; and New Deal public works programs that favored citizens over aliens.

But a minority of immigrants maintained strong emotional—and political—connections to their homelands. In the 1930s, Essex, Hudson and Bergen Counties were strongholds of the pro-Nazi groups Friends of the New Germany and the German-American Bund, which were funded by the German government. Most of the supporters of these fascist organizations were recent immigrants but not refugees from the Nazi regime, according to Warren Grover, author of *Nazis in Newark*. More established Germans were hostile toward fascism and/or feared triggering another anti-German backlash on the part of other Americans. Local politicians were embarrassed by the boisterous rallies the Friends of the New Germany held, and by 1934, the group was banned from holding large public meetings in the area. Yet these pro-Nazi Germans were a small minority within the German community in northeastern New Jersey.[291]

In 1938, Hoboken was the setting for a series of quasi-documentary short films called *Inside Nazi Germany* that were made for the newsreel serial *The March of Time*. In its newsreels, which were shown before films, *The March of Time* combined reenactments with documentary footage. In the case of the *Inside Nazi Germany* shorts, the producers had footage filmed in Germany but found that it did not reveal enough of the harshness of life under the Nazi dictatorship. And so

> The March of Time *crew went to Hoboken, N.J., where, as Dr.* [Raymond] *Fielding related in his book* The March of Time, 1935–1951 *(published in 1978), there was a German-American neighborhood whose residents were strongly anti-Nazi and happy to help raise the alarm about Hitler. Scenes of German censors going through mail, a storm trooper pressuring a housewife for a monetary contribution and so on were staged*

with the Hoboken residents and cut into the finished film alongside [Julien] *Bryan's footage.*[292]

Italians in New York and New Jersey were also divided over whether to support Benito Mussolini's fascist regime in Italy. At a time when Italians were often discriminated against in employment and housing and suffered from stereotypes of laziness and criminality, many Italian immigrants felt pride in Italy's reemergence as a great power. But Italy's increasingly aggressive foreign policy, its invasion of Ethiopia in 1936 and its support of fascist Francisco Franco in the Spanish Civil War worried many Italians and Italian Americans, who feared war between Italy and the United States.

Yet when war did eventually come at the end of 1941, Italians were not made scapegoats for their ethnic heritage as Germans had been during World War I. Many Italian Americans from Hoboken served in the U.S. Armed Forces, and the federal government again used the Hoboken piers as a major port of embarkation for servicemen going to war in Europe and Africa.

Approximately 159 Hoboken residents died fighting in World War II, including Daniel, William and Myron Wallace, for whom Wallace Elementary School at the corner of Eleventh Street and Willow Avenue is named. Anthony and James Romano were another set of brothers from Hoboken who died during the war. As in World War I, young Hoboken men found that nationality, ethnicity and religion meant little in the life-and-death struggle that was war.

But Italian American Hobokenites who survived the war came home with a changed perspective about how life in Hoboken should be. Inspired by wartime rhetoric about democracy and equality, Italian Americans overcame longstanding regional differences and organized themselves politically, joining with disaffected Irish Americans alienated from the McFeely machine. Ultimately, it was a combination of the new technology of voting machines and this coalition of Italian Americans and Irish Americans that toppled the McFeely organization in 1947. Local businessman Fred M. De Sapio became Hoboken's first mayor of Italian heritage, serving from 1947 to 1953. With the exception of John J. Grogan, the Irish American leader of the CIO Shipyard Workers who was mayor from 1953 to 1965, Italian

A crowd on Washington Street on election night, May 1947. *Hoboken Historical Museum.*

Americans held the mayor's office and often dominated the city council from the mid-1960s until David Roberts was elected mayor in 2001.[293]

The decades between World War I and World War II were a time of economic stagnation and sociocultural transition for Hoboken, as immigration restriction and the Great Depression changed the identity of Hoboken from an immigrant city dominated by Germans and Irish into an ethnic community of mostly working-class Italians and Italian Americans. After the war, a new group of people began migrating to Hoboken, and these newcomers from Puerto Rico challenged Hoboken's understanding of itself as an immigrant city.

IMMIGRATION AND MIGRATION AFTER WORLD WAR II

Puerto Ricans in Hoboken, 1945–1985

As Irish Americans and Italian Americans fought for political power in Hoboken in the late 1940s and early 1950s, the city underwent yet another demographic transformation as a new group, Puerto Ricans, began settling in Hoboken in large numbers. These newcomers faced many of the same challenges earlier immigrant groups had experienced coming to America, but the timing of Puerto Ricans' migration and the changes in American society wrought in part by earlier waves of immigration meant that Hoboken's newest ethnic group faced new difficulties and hardships in the postwar decades.

As American citizens, Puerto Ricans are not, of course, immigrants, and there were several aspects about the Puerto Rican migration that made it distinctive from that of other, earlier immigrant groups. Their status as U.S. citizens, their method of migration and the timing of their migration made the "Great Migration" of Puerto Ricans to the U.S. mainland different from that of the mass movement of Europeans to America before the First World War. Dark-skinned Puerto Ricans in Hoboken also faced additional challenges of settling into a city that had long been predominantly white.

Puerto Ricans' status as American citizens greatly facilitated their migration to the mainland as compared to other Spanish-speaking migrants from the Caribbean. When Puerto Ricans began migrating to the United States in the late 1940s and 1950s, the United States' policy of restricting immigration from Europe and largely ignoring immigration from Mexico and the rest of the Western Hemisphere was still in place. There were no quotas for immigration from the Western Hemisphere, but the distinctions of legal versus illegal immigration remained. While immigrants from other Spanish-speaking countries had to deal with the requirements of obtaining visas to legally enter the United States, Puerto Ricans moved to the mainland just as other Americans moved from one state to another.

Puerto Ricans left the island to escape high unemployment, a growing population and general poverty and to obtain higher wages and a better job market. Furthermore, lower-skilled migrants discovered that they could more easily move up the occupational ladder on the mainland than in Puerto Rico, thus achieving greater socioeconomic mobility.[294] In Hoboken, many Puerto Ricans worked in the garment and food processing industries. The Sweets Company of America, which manufactured Tootsie Roll candies in Hoboken, was an early recruiter of labor from Puerto Rico.

Unlike earlier generations of migrants, Puerto Ricans were the first group to be able to take advantage of airline travel. In the immediate aftermath of World War II, twenty-seven airlines, most of them based in Miami, established routes between San Juan and the mainland, including to New York. This new, cheap air service (a one-way ticket cost between thirty and fifty dollars depending on the airline and the destination) marked the Puerto Rican migration as one of the first large-scale air (versus sea or land) movements of people. "The airplane cost about the same and could accommodate more passengers within a week's time than could the steamships. Moreover, airplanes made a radical improvement over ships as they were able to reach their destination in a matter of six hours."[295]

In the early twentieth century, immigrants had had relatively fast transatlantic steamship travel, which facilitated seasonal migration. Italians and Greeks, especially, were called "birds of passage" for this reason.[296] For Puerto Ricans, the legal and physical ability to move from island to mainland within less than twenty-four hours simply intensified this migration experience and encouraged Puerto Ricans to see their time on the mainland as temporary. In Hoboken, this attitude of transience caused many Puerto Ricans to rent their homes and save money to buy property back in Puerto Rico (much as Italian immigrants had done before World War I) rather than saving and investing in real estate in town. Puerto Ricans also frequently returned to Puerto Rico, especially during the winter, to celebrate Christmas and New Year's with island-bound family.[297]

The Puerto Rican migration was also the first mass movement of people within the United States since African Americans began leaving the South for northern cities in large numbers in the 1920s. In 1946 alone, nearly forty thousand people left Puerto Rico, almost as many as the fifty-three thousand people who moved from the island to the mainland between 1917 (when Puerto Ricans gained U.S. citizenship) and World War II.[298] Approximately 80 percent of Puerto Ricans in the continental United States in 1940 lived in the New York City area; because of this existing Puerto Rican community and the initial prevalence of high-paying manufacturing jobs, many newcomers arriving in the 1950s settled in New York as well.

Between 1950 and 1980, New York City's Puerto Rican population grew from 254,000 to 860,000, and the city's two Italian-language radio stations switched to Spanish-language programming. New Jersey's Puerto Rican population grew as an extension of New York's: from fewer than 10,000 Puerto Ricans in 1950 to 240,000 in 1980. Approximately 50 percent of Puerto Ricans in New Jersey in 1980 lived in the urban northeastern counties of Hudson, Essex and Passaic, close to New York City.[299]

The timing of Puerto Ricans' mass migration to the mainland was also different from other groups' migrations because Puerto Ricans were moving to the mainland and, in particular, to the New York City area at a time when immigration to the United States was low and older immigrant communities were beginning to disperse from their urban neighborhoods to suburbs and assimilate into the larger American society. Between 1941 and 1950, 1.0 million people immigrated to the United States, most entering the country after World War II and many coming as refugees. Between 1951 and 1960, 2.5 million people entered the country, a significant increase when compared to the 1930s and 1940s but still quite low when compared to the mass immigration of the early twentieth century.[300]

These immigrants, as well as Puerto Ricans, entered an American society that celebrated assimilation, unity and conformity as it battled the Soviet Union in the Cold War and hunted for communists and other subversives by means of McCarthyism and the Red Scare.

Puerto Ricans' migration to the mainland also coincided with the beginnings of deindustrialization in the New York City area. In Hoboken in the 1950s and 1960s, large factories began closing and relocating to western suburbs and the South to escape high city taxes, municipal corruption, organized crime, and an inflexible urban infrastructure; densely packed, built-up Hoboken had little room for businesses looking to expand. Some large employers—such as Keuffel and Esser and the Lipton Tea Company, both of which had been in Hoboken since the mid- to late nineteenth century—finally left the city in the late 1960s. The Port of New York's adoption of containerization at its Newark and Elizabeth facilities in the late 1950s doomed Hoboken's piers to gradual obsolescence.[301]

By the late 1960s, unemployment in Hoboken was above 12 percent, and 15,000 of the city's 24,600 jobs were held by people who lived outside of the city. Hoboken residents held less than 5 percent of the city's management positions and less than 15 percent of the clerical jobs in the city. In the 1960s, Hoboken seesawed with Newark for the dubious honor of having the highest percentage of its population on welfare.[302]

This deindustrialization greatly harmed Puerto Ricans as the city's newest ethnic group:

> *The jobs which helped earlier immigrants climb the socioeconomic ladder were not available to the Puerto Ricans. Yet the members of these older ethnic groups were not always aware of this diminishment of opportunity and assumed that if the Puerto Ricans were not working, or were stuck in undesirable jobs, it was their fault, and not the economy's. The blue-collar members of the older ethnic groups were desperately holding on to the few desirable blue-collar jobs that remained in the New York area, and since they controlled the unions, they used this as a means of keeping the new immigrants out of these jobs.[303]*

Puerto Ricans moving to Hoboken settled in a city that had literally been built by German, Irish and Italian immigrants, who had immigrated before immigration restriction was imposed in the 1920s. Both the physical layout and sociocultural institutions of the city were largely fixed by the time Puerto Ricans began arriving in Hoboken. It was harder for Puerto Ricans to make their mark on Hoboken as earlier groups had done, and Puerto Ricans, for their part, were initially unsure about the depth of their commitment to life on the mainland.

Hoboken was also gradually deteriorating physically as well as economically when Puerto Ricans began moving to the Mile Square City. Most of Hoboken's housing stock had been built before 1920, and by the 1950s, much of it was falling apart. Approximately 15 percent of Hoboken dwellings shared toilets, and 27 percent only had cold water.[304] Most of these cold-water flats were tenements located near the factories in the western part of the city, west of Clinton Street, between Observer Highway and Seventh Street. Hoboken also had few parks and playgrounds and little recreational or green space. The waterfront was entirely industrial and largely closed off from public access. But despite these considerable disadvantages, Puerto Ricans in Hoboken managed to build a distinctive community based on Spanish Caribbean culture and, to a lesser extent, the Catholic Church.

In 1960, in the middle of the "Great Migration," Hoboken had 48,441 residents, but only 5,313 were from Puerto Rico. Immigrants from Italy outnumbered Puerto Ricans two to one, and when the census surveyors asked foreign-born Hobokenites what their "mother tongue" was, Italian and German, not Spanish, were most mentioned.[305] By 1970, Hoboken's Puerto Rican population had doubled (to 10,047 persons or 22 percent), while Hoboken's overall population had declined (to 45,389 residents). The next largest Spanish-speaking group in Hoboken were Cubans, who numbered 2,296 persons out of 14,322 "persons of Spanish language."[306] Within a generation, Puerto Ricans had become Hoboken's second largest ethnic group and composed the vast majority of the city's Spanish-speaking residents.

TABLE 18. FOREIGN-BORN WHITES AND THEIR COUNTRY OF ORIGIN, 1940–1960

FOREIGN-BORN WHITE	1940	1950	1960
Americas			
Canada-French	29	24	369
Canada-Other	96	112	
Mexico	7	8	13
Other Americas	58	109	848
Europe			
Italy	6,107	5,097	11,119

FOREIGN-BORN WHITE	1940	1950	1960
Germany	2,911	2,061	2,772
England	2,769	229	893
Wales	2		
Scotland	128	124	
Northern Ireland	59	1	N/A
Irish Free State (Ireland)	837	603	2,191
Norway	173	103	161
Sweden	117	70	60
Denmark	126	86	147
Netherlands	550	500	513
Belgium	258	N/A	N/A
Luxemburg	7	N/A	N/A
Switzerland	53	N/A	65
France	53	68	120
Poland	276	265	580
Czechoslovakia	123	109	127
Austria	451	408	502
Hungary	159	112	134
Yugoslavia	329	283	898
Russia (USSR)	325	246	359
Lithuania	58	34	107
Latvia	15	N/A	N/A
Finland	18	16	16
Rumania	32	22	39
Greece	110	121	216
Spain	28	N/A	N/A
Portugal	4	N/A	41
Other Europe	12	354	352
Asia	48	30	186
Other Countries	16	43	131

(U.S. Census)

TABLE 19. FOREIGN-BORN RESIDENTS AND THEIR COUNTRY OF ORIGIN, 1970

POPULATION	TOTAL
1970	45,390
Ethnicity:	
Native/native parents	27,132
Native/foreign or mixed parents	9,065
Foreign born	9,193
Origins of foreign born and children of foreign born:	
UK	348
Ireland	1,120
Sweden	64
Germany	1,165
Poland	207
Czechoslovakia	54
Austria	233
Hungary	71
USSR	184
Italy	7,835
Canada	219
Mexico	7
Cuba	2,296
Other America	941
Other and not reported	3,514

(U.S. Census, 1970)

Puerto Rican Hobokenites came from all parts of Puerto Rico, unlike Puerto Ricans in some other New Jersey communities where the Puerto Rican population was more homogeneous.[307] But as with many migrant communities, many Puerto Ricans in Hoboken had known one another or had family connections back on the island.[308]

Although Hoboken is geographically very small, different ethnic groups had long carved out certain neighborhoods and made those blocks their own. The heart of Hoboken's Puerto Rican community was Willow Avenue,

An advertisement for Tootsie Rolls, made by the Sweets Company of America in its factory in Hoboken, circa 1938–39. *Hoboken Historical Museum.*

particularly those blocks close to the Sweets Company of America's Tootsie Roll factory at Willow Avenue and Fifteenth Street. By the 1960s, the entire block of Willow Avenue between Eleventh and Thirteenth Streets consisted of Puerto Rican families, and many Puerto Ricans lived in the brownstone apartment buildings on Bloomfield and Garden Streets and Park Avenue between Eighth and Twelfth Streets. There were also clusters of Puerto Ricans living on Eighth and Ninth Streets between Park Avenue and Clinton Street and on Jefferson Street near Fifth Street.[309]

In the post–World War II period, Willow Avenue came to be viewed by all the ethnic groups in Hoboken as the "DMZ" or "demilitarized zone," dividing the "downtown" Italian neighborhoods from the "uptown" German and Irish ones.[310] Puerto Ricans thus found themselves literally and figuratively in the middle of this ethnic divide.

Like the Irish and Italians, Puerto Ricans in Hoboken were largely working-class and Roman Catholic. When Puerto Ricans began settling in Hoboken, the city already had well-established Catholic churches, with Italian, Irish and German Catholics each claiming at least one of the city's five parishes as their own territory. Puerto Ricans began attending St. Joseph's at 61 Monroe Street in the 1950s, mostly due to the outreach efforts of a Franciscan priest, Father Eugene Zwahl.

Father Zwahl was a member of the Conventual branch of the Franciscan order that had long had missions in Costa Rica, and he had learned Spanish there.[311] To minister to the growing number of Puerto Ricans in Hoboken, Father Zwahl opened the *Centro Católico* (Spanish American Catholic Center) above a hardware store on the 200 block of Washington Street in 1955 to provide recreational, religious and social welfare services to Puerto Ricans and other Spanish-speaking residents. The *Centro* remained open until 1973, when it merged with St. Joseph's parish.

Father Zwahl also began offering Spanish-language religious services at St. Joseph's, including Mass after 1965, and Puerto Ricans quickly embraced the parish and the priest as their own. "The most important achievement

Holy Names Society, St. Joseph's Church, 61 Monroe Street. *Hoboken Historical Museum.*

of Father Eugene's administration was the first efforts to bring about an amalgamation of the English and Spanish speaking communities within the parish, an awesome task at best, and seemingly insurmountable."[312]

Puerto Ricans' dedication to Father Zwahl could be seen in the fact that most Puerto Rican Catholics preferred to attend services at a church several blocks away from where they lived rather than attend Mass at Our Lady of Grace or one of the other churches closer to their homes.

In an effort to incorporate Puerto Rican Catholics into Hoboken's existing Catholic community and to keep them from attending the handful of Spanish-language Protestant churches, Father Zwahl introduced a number of Latin Catholic traditions, practices and lay organizations at St. Joseph's, including *Hijas de Maria* (Daughters of Mary, a youth organization for girls), *Madre Christiana* (Christian Mothers), *Cursillos de Cristiandad* (a spiritual retreat movement) and the Three Kings feast and procession on January 6 (the Epiphany). Father Zwahl also arranged to transport Puerto Rican Hobokenites to New York City to participate in the Archdiocese of New York's celebration of the primary Puerto Rican religious festival, the *Fiesta de San Juan* (Feast of St. John) in the 1950s and 1960s.

Daughters of Mary, St. Joseph's Church, 61 Monroe Street, at the San Juan Fiesta in New York, 1959. *Hoboken Historical Museum.*

Father Zwahl's outreach to Puerto Ricans was crucial in the development of the Puerto Rican community in Hoboken because many of the city's older residents were hostile toward the new arrivals, including many fellow Catholics.

As a city with large Irish, German and Italian Catholic populations, Hoboken had long experienced intra-faith conflict within the church over different cultural traditions and practices. The way the Catholic Church had dealt with these clashes in the past was to allow non-English-speaking immigrants to form linguistic or national parishes, where they could observe their faith in a more familiar way. So, for example, St. Francis and St. Ann's churches were built by and for Italians and practiced a particularly Italian (versus Irish or German) form of Catholicism.

But by the 1950s, the church, especially in the New York City area, had decided that the older national parish model was an antiquated approach to Catholicism, and one that both reinforced tribal ethnic identities and retarded integration, creating a more segregated church. Furthermore, church leaders now viewed such ethnic diversity as undesirable in the era of the African American civil rights movement and the Cold War. Unity, uniformity and homogeneity were now the goals of American Catholicism.

To achieve this unity and uniformity of practice, the Catholic Church, led by New York archbishop Francis J. Spellman, began promoting the creation of "integrated" parishes for Puerto Ricans. An integrated parish was a territorial or geographic parish that included at least one bilingual priest who provided services (the sermon, hymns, confession and other sacraments) in the foreign language of the targeted population. The Mass continued to be said in Latin (until Vatican II in 1965, when Mass in the vernacular language of the parish was adopted). "[But t]he English language services remained the principal services of the parish, and it was expressly intended that, as the immigrants became comfortable with English, the special second-language services would be dropped, thus producing a unified parish community as soon as possible."[313]

The church's policy of establishing national parishes was dropped in the case of Puerto Ricans, who were the first Catholic ethnic group to experience the integrated parish model. In Hoboken, St. Joseph's remained a territorial parish according to the integrated parish model, although it became the de facto "Spanish" church because of its large Puerto Rican congregation.

Although most Puerto Ricans were Catholic, a significant minority of Puerto Ricans belonged to Protestant Evangelical or Pentecostal churches.

By the 1980s, Hoboken had twelve Spanish-language Protestant churches, most of them attended by Puerto Ricans. The Latin American Pentecostal Church on First and Jackson Streets was established in 1958 and was the first church in Hoboken to hold services in Spanish.

This issue of the Spanish Mass and other religious services being offered in Spanish or English struck directly at the heart of the larger question of whether and how Puerto Ricans would integrate into mainland American society. The Spanish language has long been the basis of a unique Puerto Rican identity that is distinct from mainland American culture, which has divided people historically on the basis of skin color. "Puerto Ricans see their identity as rooted not in race but in culture and in language, and that it is this which unites Puerto Ricans of all races into one people, a people which at the same time feels bonds of brotherhood with the other nationalities that share this language and heritage, as well as with Spain, the source of both."[314] Thus, many Puerto Ricans call themselves "Spanish," referring to their primary language versus their place of origin.

Puerto Ricans' use of Spanish as the foundation of ethnic identity and their understanding of American citizenship in legalistic terms set Puerto Ricans on a collision course with other Americans, for whom the English language has long been an important measure of assimilation and for whom citizenship is both cultural as well as legal. Puerto Ricans living on the mainland thus were seen as immigrants, a Spanish-speaking minority close in culture to Dominicans and Cubans yet who happened to be U.S. citizens.

Some scholars have argued that, ironically, Puerto Ricans' status as American citizens has helped to preserve a separate Puerto Rican ethnic identity:

> *Other immigrants had to decide to become Americans, aspire to it, demonstrate proficiency in English, attend lectures on civics. After the granting of citizenship they were no longer Italians, Germans, or Poles but Americans, even if hyphenated by first generation loyalties. Italy, Germany, or Poland was now "the old country." But the Puerto Ricans, without asking for it, had been born American citizens, and entered the country as American as they needed or wanted to be for their own purposes, i.e., legally American but emotionally Puerto Rican. They were here by right and did not have to prove loyalty, undergo indoctrination, or even learn English, unless they wanted to.*[315]

The result of this was that many Puerto Ricans saw American citizenship in purely legal terms without concomitant emotional connections. "At the emotional level the Puerto Ricans thought of "Puerto Rican" and "American" as two distinct nationalities, each with its own homeland, language, culture, and flag. To leave the island for the mainland was to leave one's country and emigrate to a foreign country—of which, by an anomaly of fate, one happened to be a citizen."[316]

This "anomaly of fate" contributed to tensions between Puerto Ricans and other Americans of more recent vintage, particularly Italian Americans, in Hoboken. When Puerto Ricans began moving to Hoboken in large numbers in the late 1940s and 1950s, Italian Americans had just begun to successfully challenge the political hegemony of the city's Irish American community. As an ethnic group, Italians had been slower than other immigrant groups to assimilate and to form a new and distinctly Italian American identity. Starting out at the bottom of the socioeconomic ladder in Hoboken, as well as elsewhere in the United States, meant that Italian Americans had greater barriers to upward mobility in terms of jobs, education, political power and social status.[317]

Furthermore, although the National Origins Act of 1929 discriminated against Italians seeking to immigrate to the United States, the presence of a large number of Americans of Italian birth or ancestry meant that members of Hoboken's Italian American community could sponsor relatives for immigration. Thus, Italian immigrants continued to settle in Hoboken in the 1950s and 1960s, and after the Immigration Act of 1965 eliminated national quotas, more immigrants to the United States came from Italy than from any other country in the 1970s. The more than eleven thousand Italian-born residents in Hoboken in 1960 made up half of the city's foreign-born population and nearly one-quarter of the city's total population.[318] These new immigrants both revived and maintained the Italian American community's connection to Italian culture but also made the Italian American community appear less assimilated than it really was.

In addition, many Italian American men from Hoboken had served in World War II, an experience that allowed them to prove their loyalty to the United States (especially by fighting against fascist Italy) and exposed them to the assimilating forces of the American military. These Italian American veterans returned home both confident and defensive against any questioning of their Americanism. Puerto Ricans—with their apparent refusal to assimilate by adopting English as their primary language and their easy acquisition of American citizenship—called into question the great effort Italian Americans had expended to succeed in the United States. Anecdotally, there were more conflicts between Puerto Ricans and Italian Americans than between Puerto Ricans and any other ethnic group in Hoboken, reflecting Italian Americans' insecurities about assimilation and Puerto Ricans' casual refusal of it.[319]

Another factor in the tensions between Puerto Ricans and other Hobokenites was the issue of race. Like most people in the Caribbean and Latin America, Puerto Ricans come in all shades, and racial identity and divisions between "black" and "white" are both more fluid and less important in Puerto Rican culture than in mainland culture. But regardless of their personal racial identity, many dark-skinned Puerto Ricans found themselves living in an almost exclusively white community. Hoboken's black population jumped from 260 in 1940 to 455 in 1950 and 1,565 in 1960, and many of these "Negro" residents came from Puerto Rico.[320]

These cultural and racial differences between Puerto Ricans and other Hoboken residents manifested themselves in a variety of ways but appeared most sharply in the form of housing discrimination. Many Hoboken residents refused to rent to Puerto Ricans or charged them higher rents than they would have for persons of other ethnicities. Darker-skinned Puerto Ricans had the most trouble in this area, but even European-appearing Puerto Ricans encountered difficulties when they were discovered to be Puerto Rican and not Italian American.[321]

Puerto Ricans also experienced discrimination in Hoboken's many bars, restaurants and social clubs, with many establishments refusing to serve those who appeared "Spanish." In response, Hoboken Puerto Ricans organized their own social clubs to host dances, listen to music and eat traditional Caribbean foods. Elizabeth Forman, whose husband Jerry was a Polish American Jew from Brooklyn, opened Café Lisa, the first Puerto Rican restaurant and bar in Hoboken, in the old Clam Broth House site on the corner of Newark and River Streets. Other Puerto Rican families began opening Spanish grocery stores; the Ballester family's store, La Cocora, was on Tenth Street, while another well-known store, Bula, was on Garden Street, between First and Newark Streets. A third Spanish grocery was at Willow

Avenue and Second Street. Puerto Ricans also organized their own softball, baseball and other sports teams.[322]

Tensions between the Puerto Rican and Italian American communities in Hoboken came to a head in the early 1980s, when the Italian American mayor, Steve Cappiello, attributed a series of arson fires to an alleged Puerto Rican tradition of revenge burnings. Most of the victims of the fires between 1982 and 1985 were Puerto Ricans living in tenements in the western part of Hoboken. Cappiello's comments and his support for the gentrification of Hoboken—which hurt many working-class Puerto Rican families—caused many Puerto

The Uptown Recreation Center (No. 2), 1201 Willow Avenue, after a fire, circa 1968–72. *Hoboken Historical Museum.*

Rican Hobokenites to support Thomas Vezzetti against Cappiello in 1985. (Vezzetti defeated Cappiello in a surprising upset but died in office in 1988.)[323]

Gentrification was the main political issue in Hoboken in the 1970s and 1980s for all residents, but especially for Puerto Ricans. Hoboken's deteriorating physical infrastructure, low cost of living and proximity to New York City made the city a prime candidate for urban renewal and gentrification. As a population of mostly poor and working-class renters, Puerto Ricans were particularly vulnerable to the rising cost of living caused by gentrification.

As the city council promoted urban renewal and gentrification, some Puerto Ricans attempted to organize their fellow Spanish speakers to counter Italian Americans' domination of Hoboken's city government and to influence the redevelopment of the city but had limited success. Edwin

Duroy, who grew up in Hoboken in the 1950s, became the city's first Puerto Rican councilman, representing the Fourth Ward in the 1980s. Duroy also served on the Hoboken Board of Education in the 1990s. Lourdes Arroyo was another Puerto Rican political activist who was elected to the city council in the 1980s.[324] But Puerto Ricans have not controlled Hoboken city politics the way Irish Americans and Italian Americans have in the past, in large part because American politics is less organized around ethnic and religious identities than it was in the nineteenth and early twentieth centuries. Instead, many Puerto Ricans have voted with their feet, moving back to Puerto Rico or to nearby communities, such as Union City or Jersey City, where the cost of living is cheaper.

Although the number of Puerto Ricans in Hoboken began to drop in the 1980s, Spanish-language churches still tied former residents to Hoboken, and some churches, such as the Latin American Pentecostal Church, provided transportation to church for worshippers who lived out of town. And while some Spanish-language churches, such as Iglesia de Dios, moved to Union City to be closer to more of its parishioners, others, like Iglesia de Dios la Profecia on First Street, built new and bigger facilities on Third and Jackson Streets to meet the needs of their growing congregations. Bethesda Christian Church on Willow and Seventh Streets also stayed in Hoboken in the 1980s.[325]

In addition, the Applied Development Corporation, which began redeveloping deteriorating housing in Hoboken in the mid-1970s, enabled many working-class Puerto Ricans to stay in Hoboken by providing federally subsidized housing.[326]

Although Puerto Ricans experienced similar challenges in establishing a community in Hoboken as other, earlier immigrant groups, the city's economic decline in the 1960s hurt Puerto Ricans just at the moment when they were getting an economic foothold in the local economy. Puerto Ricans also suffered prejudice and discrimination, often because of their race, their cultural traditions and the appearance of taking their American citizenship for granted.

Conclusion

For eighty years, between 1840 and 1920, Hoboken was a city of immigrants until World War I and immigration restriction transformed the shipping industry and ended the flow of newcomers. Some of the millions of immigrants who passed through the Mile Square City decided to stay, and Hoboken quickly developed large and vibrant German, Irish, English and then Italian, Russian and Scandinavian communities. In the post–World War II period, Puerto Ricans settled in the city in large numbers.

Hoboken's Italian and Italian American communities built lasting institutions, primarily around religion. Because virtually all Italians were nominally Roman Catholic, religious festivals could also serve as community celebrations. Hoboken's Irish community was also predominantly Catholic, but Irish Americans' Catholicism emphasized service and obligation more than celebration and mysticism. Pursuing opportunities in the public sector, Irish American Hobokenites quickly came to dominate the city government. As in Jersey City and New York City, Hoboken's Irish built a powerful political organization through the local Hudson County Democratic Party, which distributed patronage jobs to thousands of Hobokenites over the course of several generations. Germans in Hoboken, however, based their community on language and the German lifestyle, which revolved around alcohol, music and social organizations. They also built German-language churches and schools, which thrived until World War I. Already experiencing intense assimilationist pressures by the early twentieth century, Germans and German Americans suffered dual blows during World War I, when both the German language and German culture were demonized. German-language newspapers folded, churches and schools switched to English and many of the *Schutzen*, *Turner* and *Sanger* Clubs disbanded. Prohibition then closed the beer gardens and saloons. With central components of the German American identity criminalized, Germans quietly assimilated. Only the German-sounding names on countless family-owned businesses revealed the extent of Hoboken's large German community.

Puerto Ricans also defined themselves primarily through language—as Spanish—but settled in Hoboken after World War II during a time of intense social pressure to assimilate and speak English. Puerto Ricans in Hoboken clashed with Italian Americans and other mainland-born Americans over questions of race, national identity and class. Deindustrialization and gentrification in the 1960s, 1970s and 1980s contributed to the shrinking of Hoboken's Puerto Rican population, and the community is increasingly elderly, with many living in subsidized housing.

Today, in 2011, Hoboken is in the middle of another demographic transformation, one that began in the 1980s and revolves around issues of socioeconomic class. Middle- and upper-middle-class people of all ethnic heritages and nationalities have begun to move to Hoboken, attracted to its nearness to New York City and its urban lifestyle. Divisions in Hoboken are now less those of nationality and ethnicity and more those of class and length of time in the community, as Hobokenites define themselves as "Old-timers" and "Newcomers." Thus, the dynamism and change that has defined Hoboken as a community since the 1840s continues.

NOTES

CHAPTER 1

1. Van Winkle, *History of Municipalities*, 302.
2. Cohn, *Mass Migration*, 62; Albion, *Rise of New York*, 339.
3. Cohn, *Mass Migration*, 127–37.
4. Ibid., 64–66; Albion, *Rise of New York*, 340, says the average ticket price was twenty dollars but ranged between fifteen and twenty-five dollars during the early packet period.
5. Hartmut Bickelmann, "The Venture of Travel," in Moltmann, *Germans to America*, 48. Bickelmann, "The Emigration Business," in Moltmann, *Germans to America*, 138, notes that self-provisioning had been prohibited in Bremen in 1832 and Hamburg in 1836 before the United States passed its American Passenger Act of 1855, which banned the practice. Agnes Bretting, "Organizing German Immigration: The Role of State Authority in Germany and the United States," in Trommler and McVeigh, *Americans and the Germans*, 32, also notes the regulation of self-provisioning at German ports.
6. Albion, *Rise of New York*, 343.
7. Ibid., 344 (for quote), 345–48.
8. Aleinikoff et al., *Immigration and Citizenship*, 149.
9. Albion, *Rise of New York*, 349–50.
10. Ibid., 338–39.

11. Data for years prior to 1906 refer to country of origin; data from 1906 to 2007 refer to country of last residence.

12. Data for Austria and Hungary not reported separately for all years during 1860 to 1869, 1890 to 1899, 1900 to 1909; from 1899 to 1919.

13. From 1899 to 1919, data for Poland included in Austria-Hungary, Germany, and the Soviet Union.

14. From 1899 to 1910, included Serbia and Montenegro. Bulgaria used to be part of Austria-Hungary until 1919.

15. Currently includes Czech Republic and Slovak Republic. Czechoslovakia was part of Austria-Hungary until it became an independent nation in 1918.

16. Prior to 1918, was part of the Russian Empire, Finland became an independent nation in 1918.

17. From 1899 to 1919, data for Poland included in Austria-Hungary, Germany, and the Soviet Union; the nation of Poland was re-established in 1918.

18. Prior to 1926, data for Northern Ireland included in Ireland.

19. Data for Norway and Sweden not reported separately until 1869.

20. From 1899 to 1919, data for Poland included in Austria-Hungary, Germany, and the Soviet Union.

21. From 1820 to 1910, included Cape Verde and Azores Islands.

22. From 1899 to 1919, data for Poland included in Austria-Hungary, Germany, and the Soviet Union.

23. From 1820 to 1920, data refer to the Russian Empire. Between 1920 and 1929, data refer to the Soviet Union.

24. From 1820 to 1910, included the Canary Islands and Balearic Islands.

25. Prior to 1926, data for Northern Ireland included in Ireland.

26. Since 1925, data for United Kingdom refer to England, Scotland, Wales and Northern Ireland.

27. Currently includes Bosnia-Herzegovina, Croatia, Macedonia, Slovenia, and Serbia and Montenegro; did not exist as a nation until 1918, when created out of Austria-Hungary.

28. Prior to 1911, data refer to British North America. From 1911, data include Newfoundland.

29. Land arrivals not completely enumerated until 1908. No data available for Mexico from 1886 to 1893.

30. Data for Jamaica not reported separately until 1953. Prior to 1953, Jamaica was included in British West Indies.

31. Included in 'Not Specified' until 1925.

32. Included in 'Not Specified' until 1925. Includes 32,897 persons returning in 1906 to their homes in the United States.

33. Burrows and Wallace, *Gotham*, 735.

34. Albion, *Rise of New York*, 336–53; Burrows and Wallace, *Gotham*, 738.

35. Albion, *Rise of New York*, 351.

36. *Report of the Commissioners of Emigration; Annual Report of the Commissioners of Emigration.*

37. *Report of the Commissioners of Emigration; Revised Laws Concerning Passengers; Annual Report of the Commissioners of Emigration.*

38. *New York Times*, August 1, 1855, 1; August 2, 1855, 4 (no headlines for either notice); "Castle Garden, How Emigrants are Treated," *New York Times*, August 4, 1855, 1; "The New Castle Garden Arrangements—Sale of Food," letter from German Society president and emigration commissioner Rudolph Garrigue, *New York Times*, August 6, 1855, 2; "New-York City, Emigration Depot, Castle Garden," *New York Times*, August 13, 1855, 8; *Annual Report of the Commissioners of Emigration.*

39. Pupin, *From Immigrant to Inventor*, 39–40. Pupin was one of the United States' rare success stories, immigrating as a young man and becoming a professor of electromechanics at Columbia University.

40. William S. Bernard, "Immigration: History of U.S. Policy," in Thernstrom, *Harvard Encyclopedia*, 488; Zolberg, *Nation by Design*, 140–45.

41. "New-York City, Emigration Depot, Castle Garden," *New York Times*, August 13, 1855, 8.

42. "Castle Garden, How Emigrants are Treated"; "Indignation Meeting, Demonstration of the Runners against the Commissioners of Emigration, Tammany Quartered on the Battery, A Loud Time under Castle Garden Walls, Capt. Rynders and O'Keefe's Speeches and a Procession," *New York Times*, August 7, 1855, 1; "Adjourned Indignation Meeting, The Runners and their Friends on the Battery, Tar Barrels, Torches, Transparencies, etc., Speeches of Theodore E. Tomlinson, Capt. Turner, D.B. Taylor, and Capt. Young, Procession through the First and Second Wards," *New York Times*, August 14, 1855, 1.

43. Garis, *Immigration Restriction*, 83–92.

44. Van Winkle, *History of Municipalities*, 287.

45. "Title and Early History," in Shaw, *History of Essex*, 1210. The Swartwout brothers failed in their farming efforts, and the land was claimed by their mortgagee, John G. Coster. This western property, known as the Coster Estate, was eventually mapped into building lots in 1860 as Hoboken began to grow.

46. Shaw, *History of Essex*, 1209–1210. Winfield, *History of the County of Hudson*, 318–19, notes that Steven auctioned off eight hundred lots over four days between March 20 and 23, 1804, and the unsold property was conveyed to the Hoboken Land & Improvement Company on May 6, 1839, after Stevens's death. See also Winfield, *Hopoghan Hackingh*, 41–49. Stevens first sailed a steam-powered ferryboat, the *Juliana*, on the Hudson in 1811–12 but soon ran afoul of New York's monopoly granted to Robert R. Livingstone and Robert Fulton. Stevens sought to get around the monopoly by inventing a "horse ferry," a paddle-wheel-type boat powered by horses, and leased such a vessel first to John, Robert and Samuel Swartwout and then to the future mayor of New York, Philip Hone, between 1817 and 1821. Hone's management was poor and purposely designed to undermine Stevens's tavern, the 76 House. Eventually, Stevens's sons bought out Hone, reintroduced steam ferryboats and then challenged the New York State legislature and Fulton and Livingstone. The monopoly was finally struck down in the important Supreme Court case *Gibbons v. Ogden* (1824).

47. Van Winkle, *History of Municipalities*, 356.

48. Ibid., 288.

49. Flynn, *Catholic Church in New Jersey*, 164.

50. In the Supreme Court case *Gibbons v. Ogden* (1824), which established the principle that the regulation of interstate transportation and commerce was the sole right of the federal government, New York State claimed that it had jurisdiction over all of New York Harbor and so had the right to grant Aaron Ogden a monopoly right to operate steamboat ferries between New York and New Jersey. In the case *Central R. Co. of New Jersey v. Jersey City*, 209 U.S. 473 (1908), the compact between the states was upheld by the court and confirmed that Jersey City and the State of New Jersey had the right to tax the land, including land under water, to the state line between New Jersey and New York. The boundaries established in the compact were the

basis of the Supreme Court decision in *New Jersey v. New York*, 523 U.S. 767 (1998) to grant New Jersey ownership of part of Ellis Island. See "The Ellis Island Verdict: The Ruling, High Court Gives New Jersey Most of Ellis Island," *New York Times*, May 27, 1998, A1.

51. Cudahy, *Over and Back*, 56.

52. Albion, *Rise of New York*, 71; Van Winkle, *History of Municipalities*, 304–10. Shaw, *History of Essex*, 1220, says North German Lloyd began providing service from Hoboken in 1863.

53. Van Winkle, *History of Municipalities*, 303–10.

54. Flagg, "From Farm and Marsh." See also Flagg, *New York Harbor Railroads*.

55. Cudahy, *Over and Back*, 56–57. The Stevens family and its real estate business, the Hoboken Land & Improvement Co., sold the ferry company to Eldridge, Roswell and Lewis in 1896–97.

56. Van Winkle, *History of Municipalities*, 309.

57. Sixth U.S. Census, *Compendium*, 22–23. The total population of Hudson County in 1840 was 9,489 persons, with 326 "free colored persons," 11 slaves and the rest white. The census began to distinguish between foreign and native born in 1850, but only at the state level. The Ninth U.S. Census of 1870 was the first census that noted the number of foreign-born residents and their nationalities in Hoboken.

58. Ninth U.S. Census, *General Tables*, 202; Eleventh U.S. Census, *General Tables*, 374–75.

59. Tenth U.S. Census, *General Population*, 452; Eleventh U.S. Census, *General Tables*, 670–77.

60. These statistics come from searches of Ancestry.com, which lists Hoboken's total population as being 2,689, not 2,668, in 1850, a difference of 21 people. The occupational analysis also comes from data collected through Ancestry.com.

61. Eleventh U.S. Census, *General Tables*, 670–77. Poland did not exist as an independent state between 1795 and 1918, and the former kingdom of Poland was divided among Russia, Austria-Hungary and Prussia. Most Polish Jews lived in the Russian section, in an area called the Pale of Settlement.

62. Espenshade, *Stone's Throw from Ellis Island*, 14, 20.

Chapter 2

63. Nadel, *Little Germany*, 41.

64. Ibid., 23–24, notes the diversity within German-speaking regions for New York City's German neighborhood, Kleindeutschland, on the Lower East Side between Fourteenth Street to the north, the Bowery and Mott Street to the west and Division and Grand Streets to the south.

65. Marianne Wokeck, "German Immigration to Colonial America: Prototype of a Transatlantic Mass Migration," in Trommler and McVeigh, *Americans and the Germans*, 5–6.

66. Vecoli, *People of New Jersey*, 88.

67. This is based on an analysis of the censuses of 1870 and 1880 by searching Ancestry.com for birthplace, as well as by the New Jersey– and New York–born children of German-born immigrants from specific states.

68. Thirteenth U.S. Census, *Population*, 151.

69. Nadel, *Little Germany*, 37–39 (segregation by sub-nationality), 48–50 (endogamy).

70. Out of 3,895 Germans who reported being born in Prussia in the U.S. Census of 1870, 1,115 lived in the First Ward, 1,020 in the Third Ward, 836 in the Fourth Ward and 830 in the Second Ward. Out of 309 Bavarians, 150 lived in the Fourth Ward, 98 in the First Ward, 31 in the Second Ward and 30 in the Third Ward. Of the 282 Badeners, 85 lived in the Second Ward, 72 in the Fourth Ward, 71 in the First Ward and 57 in the Third Ward, while of the 261 Württembergers, 86 lived in the First Ward, 74 in the Fourth Ward, 56 in the Second Ward and 48 in the Third Ward. Hoboken had 106 Saxons, 34 in the Fourth Ward, 32 in the Third Ward, 31 in the First Ward and only 7 in the Second Ward. This data is from the 1870 U.S. Census as found on Ancestry.com searching for birthplaces of Hoboken residents.

71. A close reading of the U.S. Census of 1850, for example, shows entire blocks in which Germans predominate, with no Irish residents, and vice versa. An analysis of the U.S. Census of 1880 also reveals that Germans from neighboring states preferred to live together and that southerners and northeasterners, especially Prussians and Bavarians, tended to avoid one another.

72. This is based on a sample of 181 marriages performed at St. Matthews Lutheran Church between 1875 and 1908. Virtually all of the marriages in the sample were exogamous.

73. Out of nearly 1,500 marriages performed between 1874 and 1945 at St. Joseph's Catholic Church and more than 1,200 marriages performed between 1889 and 1929 at Sts. Peter and Paul Catholic Church, only one was an interfaith marriage, between a Catholic (bride) and a "non-practicing Jew" (groom). St. Joseph's had 152 mixed marriages between Catholics and Protestants, and Sts. Peter and Paul had 251 such marriages. When Catholics married non-Catholics, they tended to marry Lutherans or Episcopalians, because Hoboken had large numbers of both denominational adherents and because these faiths were close in ritual to Roman Catholicism.

74. Van Winkle, *History of Municipalities*, 339–41.

75. Wittke, *Refugees of Revolution*, 64 (Kapff), 65 (Heinzen), 85 (von Amsberg).

76. Ibid., 332 (Rittler), 334 (Kudlich).

77. "German Political Demonstration," *New York Times*, April 13, 1854, 1.

78. Wittke, *Refugees of Revolution*, 274.

79. Vecoli, *People of New Jersey*, 116, quoting *A History of the City of Newark* (New York: Lewis Historical Publishing Co., 1913); von Katzler, "Germans in Newark," 1054.

80. Gopsills City Directory, *Jersey City, Hoboken*, 614–17, 639–43. Only nine saloon owners in 1884 had non-obvious German names, and virtually all of them were either English/American or Irish.

81. Vecoli, *People of New Jersey*, 167.

82. Ibid., 169.

83. "The Progressives vs. The Political Machine in Hoboken, 1911–1915," in Foster and Clark, *Hoboken*, 70, 74; Hoboken Board of Trade, *History of Hoboken*, 29.

84. Wittke, *Refugees of Revolution*, 301–02.

85. Ibid., 306–07; Van Winkle, *History of Municipalities*, 328–29.

86. Shaw, *History of Essex*, 1224.

87. Vecoli, *People of New Jersey*, 124–25. Vecoli notes that the number of German-language publications had dropped to fourteen in 1910 and only six in 1920.

88. Shaw, *History of Essex*, 1224–28.

89. Hoboken Board of Trade, *History of Hoboken*, 63. The U.S. Census of 1910 lists Hershensohn's name as either Hirscheasthe or Hirachensohn.

90. Nadel, *Little Germany*, 92–93; Flynn, *Catholic Church in New Jersey*, 167, notes the figure of three to four thousand German Catholics.

91. Shaw, *History of Essex*, 1224; Flynn, *Catholic Church in New Jersey*, 167.
92. Van Winkle, *History of Municipalities*, 334.
93. Vecoli, *People of New Jersey*, 118–19.
94. Shaw, *History of Essex*, 1225; Van Winkle, *History of Municipalities*, 335. Note that Brush, in Shaw, *History of Essex*, spells St. Matthew's first minister's name "Wassidlow," while Van Winkle spells it "Wossidle." I am using Wossidlo because that is the spelling St. Matthew's Lutheran uses in its church history. Brush spells Erich's name "Eiricle" and says he was from Albany, New York, while Van Winkle spells it "Eirich" and notes his difficulties with the congregation. The U.S. Census of 1880 lists a minister, Peter Erich, age fifty-two, born in Bavaria, and living at 7 Eighth Street with his family; interestingly, this was next door to the minister Henry Hafermann, age forty-eight, born in Hanover, living with his family at 6 Eighth Street (Census of 1880, Hoboken, Ward 2, District 47, 80, found on Ancestry.com searching for Hafermann). Bruckner's name is spelled several different ways in newspaper articles and in church histories: Bruecker, Bruckner, Breuchner. The census spelled it "Bruckner," so that is the spelling I am using, although the "ue" probably indicates that the correct spelling was actually Brückner. Bruckner served St. Matthew's for many years, from 1915 to 1956.
95. Hoboken Board of Trade, *History of Hoboken*, 44. I have been unable to determine Reverend Freund's first name from census records.
96. Nadel, *Little Germany*, 110–11.
97. Shaw, *History of Essex*, 1220.
98. Beck, *Tales and Towns*, 173–74, quoting Rabe.
99. Ibid., 175–76; *Halo Over Hoboken*, 28, also describes this in language very similar to Rabe's. Jersey City Directory, 1892, found through Ancestry.com, lists a Fred Schulken at 412 Washington with occupation "beer," but it is unclear whether this address was Schulken's home or business, although it certainly could have been both. *Gopsills Jersey City Directory*, 1894–95, 821, lists Frederick Schulken at 1024 Washington Street.
100. Wittke, *Refugees of Revolution*, 186.
101. "German Turners at Hoboken," *New York Times*, September 8, 1853, 8, notes the provision of New York City and Hoboken police protection for the Turners.
102. "The Affray Between the Turners and the Irish—Discharge of the Turners," *New York Times*, July 27, 1854, 8.

103. "The German Festival Yesterday," *New York Times,* June 3, 1856, 1.
104. Nadel, *Little Germany*, 107.
105. Ibid., quoting the *New Yorker Staats Zeitung*, May 25, 1850.
106. Tenth U.S. Census, *Report on the Social Statistics*, 692; Beck, *Tales and Towns*, 303–05. The Germania became the Wareing in the early 1880s and then Rialto. The census of 1880 says Germania was built in 1870.

Chapter 3

107. Quinn, *Irish in New Jersey*, 68.
108. An analysis of 270 Irish-born individuals married at Our Lady of Grace Catholic Church (OLG), Hoboken, between 1880 and 1917 revealed that the primary sending counties were Mayo (59 people or 22 percent); Galway (28 or 10 percent), Kerry (22 or .08 percent), Roscommon (19, or .07 percent) and Cavan (18 or .06 percent). The other counties sending immigrants in double digits were Clare (13 people) and Cork (12 people). The 270 individuals composed 11.25 percent of the approximately 2,400 people married at OLG between 1880 and 1917.
109. This is according to a sample of three hundred Hoboken residents who were surveyed by the U.S. Census of 1880.
110. Quinn, *Irish in New Jersey*, 102.
111. Shaw, *Immigration and Ethnicity*, 30.
112. Quinn, *Irish in New Jersey*, 84.
113. "Coronation of a Portrait of the Blessed Virgin at St. Mary's Church, Hoboken," *New York Times,* June 21, 1858.
114. Flynn, *Catholic Church in New Jersey*, 150–155, 167.
115. Ibid., 155–57. The First Dutch Reformed Church was formed in 1850, and the congregation later built a church on Bloomfield Street between Eighth and Ninth Streets. Hoboken Board of Trade, *History of Hoboken*, 52–53.
116. Flynn, *Catholic Church in New Jersey*, 161–164. Our Lady of Grace School and St. Mary's Hospital, now the Hoboken University Hospital, were built in 1865.
117. Flynn, *Catholic Church in New Jersey*, 164–65.
118. Shaw, *History of Essex*, 1224.

119. Vecoli, *People of New Jersey*, 114–15.

120. Van Winkle, *History of Municipalities*, 333.

121. Flynn, *Catholic Church in New Jersey*, 167–71.

122. Ibid., 169–71.

123. Quinn, *Irish in New Jersey*, 144; Kathleen Neils Conzen, "Germans, Churches, Schools and the Press," in Thernstrom, *Harvard Encyclopedia*, 417–19 (Cahenslyism).

124. Vecoli, *People of New Jersey*, 112–13. Wigger served as bishop of Newark from 1881 to 1901.

125. Flynn, *Catholic Church in New Jersey*, 167, notes Wigger's efforts to find a suitable German-speaking priest to minister to Hoboken's German Catholics in the early 1870s.

126. This is according to an analysis of the censuses of 1860 and 1870, as well as Gopskills City Directory, 614–617, 639–43. "Robert Nicle" probably spelled his name "Nichols," but "Nicle" is how the census enumerator spelled it.

127. Ninth U.S. Census of 1880, found on Ancestry.com; also Gopskills City Directory, 614; Jersey City City Directory.

128. Gopskills City Directory, 616; Jersey City City Directory. The Thirteenth U.S. Census of 1910 shows a Thomas Normoyle, age forty-four, born in Ireland in 1866, living on Willow Avenue in the Third Ward with wife Constance, twenty-two-year-old son John and Constance's brother, John Reanon.

129. Gopskills City Directory, 816–22. For the first time, there were also some Italian-sounding names of bar owners, such as Aniello Lanzetta, Joseppe Lucianao, C. Marrone, John Richetto and John Zuvella. All of these men lived in the far western part of town, on Grand, Adams and Jefferson Streets.

130. Quinn, *Irish in New Jersey*, 108.

131. Ibid., 107–09; Sobel and Raimo, *Biographical Directory*. New Jersey's state constitution of 1844 stipulated that the governor serve three-year terms; this was lengthened to four years in the 1947 state constitution. Hudson County had 1,011 black residents (42 of them in Hoboken, the rest in Jersey City), according to the Ninth U.S. Census, *General Tables*, 202.

132. Vecoli, *People of New Jersey*, 164.

133. Ibid., 165.

134. Approximately 74 out of 138, or 53 percent, of Irish male heads of household were laborers, according to the U.S. Census of 1850.

135. This is according to a careful reading of all Irish-born males living in Hoboken who were surveyed by the U.S. Census of 1860.
136. Vecoli, *People of New Jersey*, 87.

CHAPTER 4

137. U.S. Supreme Court, *Henderson v. Mayor of City of New York*, 92 U.S. 259 (1875), http://caselaw.lp.findlaw.com/cgi-bin/getcase. pl?court=us&vol=92&invol=259 (accessed February 12, 2011).
138. Garis, *Immigration Restriction*, 84–97.
139. New York State Department of Labor, *Bureau of Industries*, Fourth Annual Report, 276–280; Fifth Annual Report, 23–28. In 1914, the head tax was $4; by 1915, the U.S. Bureau of Immigration had a surplus of $9 million in head tax revenues, which went directly into the U.S. Treasury.
140. Van Winkle, *History of Municipalities*, 304, 305.
141. Wyman, *Round-Trip America*, 23-25, notes that the transatlantic trip usually took about ten days because ships did not always go directly from Europe to eastern U.S. ports.
142. For example, see "*Imperator* Delayed by Mob of Visitors, Big Hamburg-American Liner an Hour Late Starting Back on Second Trip," *New York Times*, July 20, 1913, 11.
143. The 1900 pier fire was so dramatic that several postcards were made of the fire and its aftermath. Many copies of these postcards are now in the collection of the Hoboken Historical Museum.
144. Although some steamship lines used the terms "steerage" and "third class" interchangeably in the pre–World War I era, steerage here refers to the temporary bunk or cot sleeping arrangements common in the mid-nineteenth century, while third class refers to the shared cabins and better food and amenities available in the early twentieth century. That being said, some ships had both third and steerage classes. U.S. Citizenship and Immigration Services, "This Month in Immigration History: April 1912," U.S. Department of Homeland Security, http://uscis.gov/graphics/aboutus/history/April1912; Smith and Herring, Bureau of Immigration. Between 1892 and 1903, the Office of the Superintendent of Immigration was located in the Treasury Department. In 1903, the

Bureau of Immigration was created and placed in the Department of Commerce and Labor. In 1906, the office was reorganized as the Bureau of Immigration and Naturalization, and in 1913, the divisions were separated again and placed in the new Department of Labor.

145. Steiner, *On the Trail*, 64–72.

146. Kraut, *Silent Travelers*, 66.

147. "Immigration: History of U.S. Policy," in Thernstrom, *Harvard Encyclopedia*, 491.

148. *Report of the Commission of Immigration*. Although Franks was listed as being "of Hoboken," he was listed in the U.S. Census of 1910 as living in West Orange. All the members of the commission donated to support the agency, as well as Carnegie, Rockefeller, M. Taylor Pyne, Sidney Colgate, Mrs. Caroline B. Alexander, Miles Tierney, Russell Colgate, Richard M. Colgate, Mrs. William Barr, J. William Clark, Mrs. S. Hartshorn, Allison Dodd and Percy R. Pyne. Sidney Colgate and Caroline Alexander were members of the NACL's New York–New Jersey Committee, and M. Taylor was the NACL secretary.

149. *Report of the Commission of Immigration*, 23. A hackman was the driver of a hack, which is short for hackney carriage, a horse-drawn vehicle.

150. *Report of the Commission of Immigration*, 24.

151. Ibid., 24–25.

152. Ibid., 26. In this instance, the commissioners were aware of the porter's alleged reputation before the reported incident because a German man had filed a complaint of seduction of his daughter with the commission after traveling to Hoboken from Nebraska with the intention of killing the porter.

153. *Report of the Commission of Immigration*, 27.

154. Ibid., 27–28; Howe, *Confessions of a Reformer*. Chapter 25 discusses the exploitation of immigrants on both sides of the Hudson in the early twentieth century.

155. *Report of the Commission of Immigration*, 28–29; New York State Department of Labor, *Bureau of Industries*, First Annual Report, 53 (for quote).

156. *A Nice Tavern*, 6.

157. *Report of the Commission of Immigration*, 28–29; New York State Department of Labor, *Bureau of Industries*, First Annual Report, 43, 48–49, notes the related problem of luggage transfer.

158. *Report of the Commission of Immigration*, 28.

159. *A Nice Tavern*, 7.

CHAPTER 5

160. Analysis of the U.S. Censuses of 1860 and 1870. In 1860, three Italian heads of household lived in the First Ward, three in the Second Ward and two in the Third Ward (this includes one female Italian head of household, hotel keeper Ambrosia P. Calabretta, who listed her birthplace as Naples). In 1870, out of twenty-eight Italian-born men (and boys), three lived in the First Ward, none in the Second Ward, ten in the Third Ward and thirteen in the Fourth Ward. In 1870, Hoboken had fifty-four Italian-born residents, nearly all of them adults.

161. Twelfth U.S. Census, *Population*, 796–99. In this era, the census distinguished between immigrants from French-speaking Quebec and the rest of Canada.

162. This is based on an analysis of marriage records at St. Ann's Church in Hoboken between 1919 and 1946. St. Joseph's was the first Italian Catholic church in Hoboken, but its marriage records, which begin in 1874, do not list which region of Italy parishioners were from, only "Italy," whereas towns and counties of Ireland are noted.

163. Eleventh U.S. Census, *General Tables*, 670–73; Thirteenth U.S. Census, *Population*, 144–45.

164. Vecoli, *People of New Jersey*, 220.

165. Jersey City, *Hoboken Directory*, 1915, 1612. Out of the forty-eight bakers in Hoboken in 1915, nineteen were Italian; the rest had German-sounding names. Carlo Guastaferro had immigrated to Hoboken from San Giuseppi Vesuviano, Naples, Italy, in the early 1900s and moved from 412 Adams Street to 95 Washington Street in the late 1990s.

166. "Italo Marcioni," in Cavaioli et al., *Italian American Experience*, 359.

167. Bierbaum, "Hoboken, a Come-Back City," 75.

168. Vecoli, *People of New Jersey*, 220.

169. Gopskills City Directory, 1884–85, 615; 1886–87, 245; 1894–95, 818; 1884–1885, 639–43; Thirteenth U.S. Census, *Hoboken Ward 3*, 24–25, found on Ancestry.com searching for John Podesta. The only other liquor dealer with an Italian-sounding name in 1885, Marco Bulat, owned an establishment at 142 Adams and lived next door to John Podesta at 328 Adams, but he was born in Austria.

170. Gopskills City Directory, 1894–95, 816–22.

171. Boyd's City Directory, Jersey City and Hoboken, 1904–05, 816–25.

172. Jersey City, *Hoboken Directory*, 1915, 1812–14; Thirteenth U.S. Census, *Hoboken Ward 2*, 6. John Podesta and his family lived at 103 Fourth Street. By 1910, the John Podesta family had moved to 927 Hudson Street, one of the nicest addresses in Hoboken, according to the Fourteenth U.S. Census, *Hoboken Ward 2*, 17, found on Ancestry.com. Angelo Podesta and his family lived nearby at 931 Hudson Street in 1910.

173. Burrows and Wallace, *Gotham*, 1124–26.

174. "History of St. Francis Church," www.stfrancishoboken.com/thechurch.html.

175. "The History of St. Ann's Parish," www.st-annchurch.com/default.asp?contentID=31.

176. Vecoli, *People of New Jersey*, 224.

177. Ibid., 225.

178. Ibid., 226–27.

179. "The History of St. Ann's Parish"; www.hobokenitalianfestival.com/html/society.htm.

180. The Madonna Dei Martiri festival was held at St. Ann's until 1938, when it temporarily moved outdoors to Moonachie before returning to St. Ann's in 1946. In 1948, the society moved itself and the Madonna statue to St. Francis Church. The society's headquarters was originally located at 230 Willow Avenue between its incorporation in 1927 and 1950, when it moved to 332 Adams Street.

181. "Bullets Fly Thick in a Hoboken Riot, Accidental Killing of a Boy Arouses Italians, Who Open Fire on the Police," *New York Times*, May 6, 1909. The riot and shootout began after grocery wagon driver Luigi Licassi accidentally ran over four-year-old Michael Barracano of 409 Monroe Street. After fleeing the scene of the accident, Licassi and his boss, Lupo Lapresta of New York City, returned to Hoboken and went to the police, asking for officers to accompany them back to the stable, possibly out of fear of retribution by the upset parents and neighbors. When Licassi, Lapresta and two Irish American police officers arrived at Monroe Street, they were shot at from several houses.

182. Govorchin, *Americans from Yugoslavia*, 41, 74, 116, 143.

183. Hoboken Board of Trade, *History of Hoboken*, 55.

184. Eleventh U.S. Census, *General Tables*, 671.

185. Fourteenth U.S. Census, *Statistics of Population*, 796–99.
186. Thirteenth U.S. Census, *Population*, 144–45.
187. Ibid.
188. Ibid., 151.
189. Ibid.
190. Hoboken Board of Trade, *History of Hoboken*, 28–29.
191. "The Progressives vs. The Political Machine in Hoboken," in Foster and Clark, *Hoboken*, 63–79. Clark notes on page 72 that "during his political career, Paddy Griffin was able to amass a fortune estimated at two million dollars including a mansion in Monmouth Beach, and a summer home in Spring Lake."
192. Ibid.
193. Luebke, *Bonds of Loyalty*, 193, argues that a factor in Germans' support for the Republican Party was that Italians tended to vote Democratic, but many Italians also voted Republican in reflection of their antipathy for the Irish. A voter's religious affiliation was also a factor, with Catholics tending to vote Democratic. Vecoli argues that Italians in Hudson County tended to vote for whoever was the strongest, so for the Republicans in Newark but for the Democrats in Jersey City (p. 227).
194. "The Progressives vs. The Political Machine in Hoboken," in Foster and Clark, *Hoboken*, 63–79.

CHAPTER 6

195. Remington had four thousand workers in Hoboken during World War I, American Lead Pencil had fourteen hundred workers and Tiejen and Lang had nineteen hundred workers. Van Winkle, *History of Municipalities*, 339–40.
196. Furer, "'Heaven, Hell, or Hoboken,'" 147.
197. "An Interpretation of Hoboken's Population Trends, 1856-1970," in Foster and Clark, *Hoboken*, 47–62. The city fought the federal government for years to be reimbursed for its loss of tax revenues, finally gaining some compensation in 1950.
198. Van Winkle, *History of Municipalities*, 310.
199. "An Interpretation of Hoboken's Population Trends," in Foster and Clark, *Hoboken*, 51.

200. "War Charity Fete on the Vaterland, Giant Hamburg-American Liner Houses a Fancy Dress Festival, To Aid Central Powers," *New York Times*, November 5, 1916, 11. The *Times* reports that approximately $7,000 was raised and that tickets were a pricey $10 each.

201. The declaration of war was the culmination of events in early 1917, beginning with Germany's announcement of the resumption of unrestricted submarine warfare on January 31. The United States severed diplomatic relations with Germany on February 3, and by March 20, Wilson's war cabinet had voted for a declaration of war. President Wilson requested such a declaration on April 2, and Congress issued the declaration on April 6. The United States declared war on Austria-Hungary on September 8, 1917.

202. "Eight Taken Here as German Spies, Secret Service Begins Roundup of Enemy Aliens Not Deemed Safe to be at Large," *New York Times*, April 7, 1917, 3; "19 More Taken As German Spies, Dr. Karl George Frank, Former Head of Sayville Wireless, Among Those Detained. Six Taken to Ellis Island. In Eleventh Street Rooming House Police Find Suspects and Supply of Arms," *New York Times*, April 8, 1917, 1.

203. Bruckner had come to the United States in 1911 and had become the pastor of St. Matthew's in 1915 after the previous pastor, the Reverend Alexander Richter, suffered a nervous breakdown as a result of being in Germany when the war started in August 1914. "Eight Taken Here as German Spies, Secret Service Begins Roundup of Enemy Aliens Not Deemed Safe to be at Large," *New York Times*, April 7, 1917, 3.

204. "Takes Some Teutons from Ellis Island, Eight Enemy Aliens Start for Fort Oglethorpe, Ga., with Others from Interior," *New York Times*, August 28, 1917, 7.

205. "Gloom Over Hoboken As Residents Cower Under Uncle Sam's Eye, Shocked Amazement Caused by Eviction of Max Muller and Fred Jarka, Steamship Men, and Restrictions Imposed by Troops Puzzle Them," *New York Telegram*, April 2, 1917, found in *World War I Scrapbook*, Hoboken Public Library.

206. "19 More Taken As German Spies," 1; Millman, *The Detonators*, 21–24, also discusses this, and on pages 41–44, 56–58, it discusses Koenig's espionage activities, as does Witcover, *Sabotage at Black Tom*, 59–66.

207. "German Arrested for Making Bombs, Deadly Missiles and High Explosives Found in his Room in a Hoboken Hotel, Plot Stories Are

Denied, No Proof Found of Rumors That Prisoner Had Intended to Attack President Wilson," *New York Times*, March 6, 1917, 1; "All Spy Arrests Now Kept Secret, Prisoners Go Direct to Ellis Island Without Any Proceedings in Court, Arrest in Customs House, Man Seeking Job on German Ship Gives Forged Letter-Suspects Taken in Mount Vernon," *New York Times*, April 13, 1917, 3; Witcover, *Sabotage at Black Tom*, 210.

208. "German in Jail Who Saw Troops Depart, Man of Evident Culture Labored on Pier When Transports Carrying Pershing Force Sailed," *New York Times*, July 14, 1917, 3; "Arrested as Bomb Maker, German Machinist Accused in Part in Hoboken Ship Plots," *New York Times*, June 10, 1917, 4.

209. German chemist Walter Scheele had a bomb-making factory in Hoboken in 1915–17, and he also trained the sailors on the moored *Frederick Der Grosse* (Frederick the Great) to make timed explosive devices, which were smuggled aboard British ships in the guise of cigars. Millman, *The Detonators*, 21–24, 90–96; Witcover, *Sabotage at Black Tom*, 89–91. See also "Wall-St Explosion Laid to Gelatin, Dr. Walter T. Schleele, Explosive Expert, Says Blasting Material Did It," *New York Times*, October 16, 1920.

210. "Germans Here Quick to Back President, Citizens of Teutonic Descent Pledge Undivided Loyalty to Our Government, No Dissenting Voice Here, Liederkranz Committee to Co-Operate with German Hospital in Planning Joint Activities," *New York Times*, April 7, 1917, 5.

211. "27 Ships Taken Here, Government May Use Liners Later as Troop Transports, Vaterland Not Damaged, Soldiers Aid Collector Malone in Removing 1,100 Officers and Men to Ellis Island, Took Seizure Stoically, Sang and Cheered as They Left Piers—Women and Children Detained, May Be Released," *New York Times*, April 7, 1917, 1. The article notes that the women and children would probably be sent back to Germany rather than held indefinitely at Ellis Island. See also "Seizure of German Ships Takes Place Without Difficulty," *Hudson Observer*, April 6, 1917, found in *World War I Scrapbook*, Hoboken Public Library.

212. "Army Put in Charge of Piers in Hoboken, Waterfront Used by Teuton Lines to be a Government Shipping Base. Mayor Reassures Germans, May Live in the District So Long as They Are Orderly—Strict Rules for Saloons," *New York Times*, April 20, 1917, 1.

213. Van Winkle, *History of Municipalities*, 316, quoting "With the Army at Hoboken."

214. "Government Buys 3 Hoboken Piers of German Line, United States Acquires Property of Hamburg-American Company Here," *New York Times*, May 4, 1919.

215. Furer, "'Heaven, Hell, or Hoboken,'" 149; "27 Ships Taken Here, Government May Use Liners Later as Troop Transports, Vaterland Not Damaged, Soldiers Aid Collector Malone in Removing 1,100 Officers and Men to Ellis Island, Took Seizure Stoically, Sang and Cheered as They Left Piers—Women and Children Detained, May Be Released," *New York Times*, April 7, 1917, 1; Albert Bushnell Hart, "Seizure of German Ships, Distinguished Harvard Professor Urges the United States to Take Them Over Without Any Delay," *New York Times*, April 1, 1917, SM1.

216. Van Winkle, *History of Municipalities*, 318.

217. Ibid., 310–13. Van Winkle notes that the United States also had access to British, French and Italian ships, for a total of 173 transatlantic liners.

218. "Wilson Asks Title to German Piers, Congress Urged to Legislate to Acquire Government-Controlled Hoboken Docks, Senators Seek Reason, Request Help Up in Committee, Pending Reply—Palmer Explains Sales of Enemy Property," *New York Times*, March 6, 1918, 7; "Move to Make Big German Concerns American-Owned, Amendments Reported to Senate Strike at Interests Close to Kaiser's Government, Hoboken Piers Included, Authority Given to Sell These, When Acquired, and Any Other Great Property Held, Values Exceed a Billion, Tremendous Advantage to This Country in Post-War Trade Seen in Acquisitions," *New York Times*, March 8, 1918, 1; "Vote to Root Out Financial Power of Germany Here, Senators Are Unanimous for Drastic Program in Seizure and Sale of Investments, May Never Be Returned, Treaty of 1799 Is Held to Be No Bar to the Action Now Contemplated, Taking Over of German Terminals at Hoboken Is Agreed to Without Debate," *New York Times*, March 12, 1918, 1 (quote). Also, "Authorizes Sale of Hoboken Piers, House Agrees to Amendment Giving Full Power to Dispose of Enemy Property," *New York Times*, March 27, 1918, 15. The term "Junkerism" refers to the Junkers of Prussia, aristocratic landowners whom Americans accused of fostering a tradition of militarism.

219. "Government Takes Over all Dock Work, Conferees Decide on Control of Employment of Stevedores in Every Port, Hope to Eliminate Delays, Office at Battery Here Will Have Branches, T.V. O'Connor Is Placed in Charge," *New York Times*, June 8, 1918, 7.

220. "Now Included in the Restricted Zone. To Issue Few Permits, Hundreds of Germans Now Employed on the River Will Now Lose Their Jobs," *New York Times*, May 7, 1917, 8.

221. "Enemy Alien Migration," *New York Times*, November 22, 1917, 4.

222. "Bar All German-Americans, Citizens of Teutonic Birth Discharged from Hoboken Piers," *New York Times*, July 10, 1917, 2; "Waterfront Closed to Enemy Aliens, Residents and Employees Included in Regulations Effective Today, Arrest for Disobedience, Marshal McCarthy Calls on All Good Citizens to Notify Him of Violations," *New York Times*, July 11, 1917, 5; "Quiet Control of the Germans in New York, No Disturbance and Only Slight Display of Prejudice Mark Readjustment of Living Conditions Among Thousands of Aliens," *New York Times*, July 29, 1917, 56.

223. "Graft Charged by Teutons, Say They Are Forced to Pay to Get into Marshal's Office," *New York Times*, June 9, 1917, 2.

224. Furer, "'Heaven, Hell, or Hoboken,'" 168.

225. Hannah Fischer, "American War and Military Operations Casualties: Lists and Statistics," Knowledge Services Group; Kim Klarman and Mari-Jana "M-J" Oboroceanu, Congressional Research Service, updated June 29, 2007, http://72.14.205.104/search?q=cache:QrSH4fUHvOwJ:ftp.fas.org/sgp/crs/natsec/RL32492.pdf+American+casualties+first+world+war&hl=en&ct=clnk&cd=10&gl=us.

226. Van Winkle, *History of Municipalities*, 318.

227. "Seek Officers' Quarters, War Camp Community Committee Tells of Needs Here," *New York Times*, March 19, 1918, 11; "Get German Sailors' Home, Army Officials Take Possession of House in Hoboken," *New York Times*, March 12, 1918, 13.

228. Van Winkle, *History of Municipalities*, 313.

229. Coffman, *War to End All Wars*, 328–29; Kennedy, *Over Here*.

230. "Army Put in Charge of Piers in Hoboken, Waterfront Used by Teuton Lines to be a Government Shipping Base, Mayor Reassures Germans, May Live in the District So Long as They Are Orderly, Strict Rules for Saloons," *New York Times*, April 20, 1917, 1.

231. "Rumor Mongers Caught in Net of Government, Twelve, Found by Secret Service, Must Explain Origin of Disturbing Reports. Enemy Aliens Responsible, Washington Authorities Determined to Put an End to Widespread Propaganda," *New York Times*, June 13, 1917, 1.

232. "61 Hoboken Saloons Must Close at Ten, General Bell's Order Affecting Waterfront Places Sent to Mayor, Who Tells Owners, Zone May Be Extended, Single Violation to Result in Shutting-Up All Places During Period of War, Fifty-nine Germans Affected," *New York Times*, July 4, 1917, 6.

233. "Disregard Bell's Order, Hoboken Saloon Keepers Say They Will Await Official Closing Notice," *New York Times*, July 5, 1917, 9; "Hoboken Saloon Men Keep Open to Music, Waterfront Enjoys Bands and Singers While Mayor and Police Do Not Interfere," *New York Times*, July 7, 1917, 6; "Hoboken Still Defiant, Riverfront Saloons Open Until Midnight, Despite Military Order," *New York Times*, July 8, 1917, 6.

234. "Mandate to Close All Hoboken at Ten, City Commissioners Will Pass Sweeping Saloon Ordinance by Order of Government, Ends Defiance of Army, Every Drinking Place in the City Will Fall Under Ban First Applied to Waterfront Only," *New York Times*, July 11, 1917, 12.

235. "Hoboken Awaits Mandate, Dispute Between Saloons and Army Now Up to Washington," *New York Times*, July 13, 1917, 6.

236. "Hoboken Refuses to Close Up Early, Rejects Army Officer's Request to Shut up River Front Saloons at 10 PM., Defies Threat of Force, Adopts Midnight Rule for the City at Large and Forbids River Front Sunday Sales," *New York Times*, July 12, 1917, 4.

237. "Hoboken Awaits Mandate, Dispute Between Saloons and Army Now Up to Washington," *New York Times*, July 13, 1917, 6.

238. "Orders Hoboken Bars Closed to Soldiers, Mayor Shuts One Place and Gives Other Saloon Keepers a Week in Which to Reform," *New York Times*, August 2, 1917, 11; "German Arrested for Making Bombs, Deadly Missiles and High Explosives Found in His Room in a Hoboken Hotel, Plot Stories Are Denied, No Proof Found of Rumors That Prisoner Had Intended to Attack President Wilson," *New York Times*, March 6, 1917, 1, notes that the Commercial Hotel was located at 212 River Street.

239. "Wires President to Save Saloons, Hoboken's Mayor Asks Wilson to Defer the Federal Closing Order. 338 Bars Are Affected, Enforcement of Half-Mile Clause Will Make the Entire City Dry," *New York Times*, September 30, 1917, 8; "168 Hoboken Saloons Dark, Dry Zone May Be Extended to Include 112 More," *New York Times*, November 4, 1917, 12; "50 More Saloons Closed, Dry Zone Extended Again into Hoboken and Weehawken," *New York Times*, November 6, 1917, 11.

240. "May Charge Treason in Theft of Army Sugar, Ex-Alderman of Hoboken Accused of Buying and Selling Stolen Supplies," *New York Times*, August 2, 1917, 3.

241. Furer, "'Heaven, Hell, or Hoboken,'" 154.

242. Ibid., 154–55, 157–58.

243. "Hoboken Schools Drop German as a Study, Teacher of That Language Becomes Director of the Bureau of Americanization," *New York Times*, September 8, 1917, 4.

244. "Soldiers Arrest 200 in Raid in Hoboken, Hunt Out Enemy Aliens in a Thorough Search of River Street Resorts," *New York Times*, November 20, 1917, 1; "Waterfront Patrol Takes 4,000 Men, Regulars Expected to Take Over Guardianship of Piers with Local Aid," *New York Times*, November 21, 1917, 9, notes Struntz's arrest; "New Enemy Migration," *New York Times*, November 22, 1917, 4; "Barred Zone Shut to Rich Germans, Must Vacate Luxurious Downtown Offices and Quit Trade Near the Waterfront, 'Influence' Found Useless, More Enemy Aliens Arrested—Enlightening Letter Found on Spy Suspect, Naturalization Inquiry, Circumstances Under Which Austrians Were Admitted to Citizenship to be Looked Into," *New York Times*, November 22, 1917, 4; "Military Guard Put in Control of River Fronts, Armed Soldiers to Go on Duty on City Piers at Midnight Tonight. Will Shoot Trespassers, Unidentified Persons, Whether Citizens or Aliens, Must Not Enter Barred Zones," *New York Times*, November 25, 1917, 1; "No Soldiers Sent to Guard Piers; Only Police There, Program as to Barred Zones Changed Here to Take in 'Vital Points' Only. Washington Is Puzzled, Can't Understand Failure to Carry Out the Federal Instructions," *New York Times*, November 26, 1917, 1.

245. "City's German List Holds 39,596 Names, Total Registered is 7,000 Less Than Expected by Marshal McCarthy, Other Subjects Known, Prompt Round Up of Those Who Failed to Record Themselves Under Law Is Looked For," *New York Times*, February 14, 1918, 8.

246. "Dutch Refuse Ship Transfer on Allied Terms, Demand Guarantees That Vessels Won't Be Used for Troops or Munitions, Seizures Likely Today," *New York Times*, March 19, 1818, 1; "Government Buys 3 Hoboken Piers of German Line, United States Acquires Property of Hamburg-American Company Here," *New York Times*, May 4, 1919, notes the navy's use of the Scandinavian Line's piers during the war.

247. "Army to Clean Up Hoboken," *New York Times*, March 8, 1918, 7.

248. "New York Loan Total Reaches $504,230,700," *New York Times*, April 27, 1918, 4, initially reported that Hoboken residents had bought $2,255,750 worth of bonds, only 55 percent of their $4,194,600 quota. Also see "Loan Subscribed; Drive Is On Today for Big Surplus, $2,940,640,400 Total Officially Reported Without Yesterday's Subscriptions, Record Mark on Thursday, Chicago and New England Districts Are the Latest to Go Over the Top," *New York Times*, May 4, 1918, 1; "New York District Exceeds Quota; Total for Loan Now $926,971,000, Number of Subscribers Here 4,000,000, Double That of Second Campaign—City Also 'Over the Top' and Unfurls Honor Flag," *New York Times*, May 5, 1918, 1.

249. "Kaiser's Head on Nickels, Police Search for Distributors of Altered Coins in Hoboken," *New York Times*, May 2, 1918, 13.

250. Enemy Badly Battered, Registered German Alleged to Have Spoken Too Freely," *New York Times*, June 3, 1918, 11.

251. "Killed in Row Over War, Longshoreman Charged with Murder of Hoboken Pressman," *New York Times*, July 16, 1918, 6.

252. "Books of Dry Dock Corporation Seized, Federal Authorities Seek Evidence that Young Men Evade Draft Law by Working There," *New York Times*, June 26, 1918, 13.

253. "Begin New Roundup of Enemy Aliens, Several Arrests Made and at Least Two Wealthy Germans Under Investigation, Otto Bollmann Arrested, Had Gone Out of His Way to Show Loyalty to Kaiser—Swede Charged with Sedition," *New York Times*, July 6, 1918, 7.

254. "Seize 20,000 Here in Slacker Search, Men Between 21 and 31 Halted in Streets and Registration Cards Demanded, 12,000 Taken in New Jersey, 200 Proven Slackers Sent as Prisoners to Governors Island and Upton," *New York Times*, September 4, 1918, 1. Also "60,187 Men Taken in Slacker Raids, Chief De Woody Reports Cases of 16,505 Were Referred Back to Local Boards. Few Willfully Delinquent, 500 'Proved Slackers' in Manhattan and 256 in Brooklyn Sent to Camps," *New York Times*, September 8, 1917, 9.

255. "Grip Now Sweeping Forty-Three States, Drastic Steps Taken Through-out the Nation to Check the Epidemic, Stop Public Meetings, Theatres Ordered to Close in Washington and All Gatherings are Barred in Pennsylvania," *New York Times*, October 4, 1918, 24. "Grip" or "grippe" was another term for influenza.

256. Van Winkle, *History of Municipalities*, 315.

CHAPTER 7

257. Garis, *Immigration Restriction*, 142–43; Daniels, *Guarding the Golden Door*, 49. Please also see Department of Homeland Security, Bureau of Immigration and Citizenship, Quota Law of May 19, 1921 (42 Statutes-at-Large 45) and Act of May 11, 1922 (42 Statutes-at-Large 540).

258. Massachusetts Department of Education, *Annual Report*, 13–17.

259. Garis, *Immigration Restriction*, 169–202, 183 (quote); Daniels, *Guarding the Golden Door*, 51–53.

260. Garis, *Immigration Restriction*, 256–62, see esp. table "Comparison of Quota for 1923–24 with Quota for 1924–25." Germany's quota for 1924–25 was 51,227; Britain's was 34,007; and Ireland's was 28,567.

261. Jersey City, *Hoboken Directory*, 1915, 1717; Polk's City Directory, *Jersey City and Hoboken*, 1925–26, 1313.

262. The lessees in 1922 were the Cosmopolitan Steamship Company, the Munson Line and the Panama Steamship Company. All of the stock in the Panama line was owned by the federal government. "Asks U.S. to Pay Tax on 6 Hoboken Piers, City is Heard on Senate Committee on Claims for $1,500,000 Loss by Seizure," *New York Times*, July 16, 1922. The City of Hoboken consistently argued that because the piers were no longer in "public use," and because the federal government was realizing millions in rent on the piers and running them like a private business, the federal government should pay tax on the piers even though they were now public property. For evidence, Hoboken pointed to the federal government's compensation of local communities that lost tax dollars when the United States created forest preserves.

263. "Over Half Million in Uncollected Taxes on Hoboken Pier Property," *Jersey Observer*, July 29, 1920, found in *World War I Scrapbook*, Hoboken Public Library. See also "To Grant Relief to the City of Hoboken, New Jersey," in *Hearings before the Committee on the Judiciary, House of Representatives, 66th Congress, Third Session, Serial 27, February 21, 1921* (Washington, D.C.: Government Printing Office, 1921); "Claims of the City of Hoboken, NJ," in *Hearings before a subcommittee of the Committee on Claims, U.S. Senate, 67th Congress, Second Session, pursuant to S. Res 254, to Investigate the Claims of the City of Hoboken, NJ, for Losses as a Result of the Occupation by the United States of Certain Docks, July 15 and Aug. 8, 1922* (Washington, D.C.: Government

Printing Office, 1922). The German piers represented about 15 percent of the taxable property in Hoboken by 1917.

264. "Hoboken Gets $105,000 Pier Taxes, North German Lloyd Arrearges for 1918 Are Paid by Palmer," *Hoboken Dispatch*, February 23, 1921, found in *World War I Scrapbook*, Hoboken Public Library.

265. The state granted Hoboken $136,376.07 in 1924 for 1919 and 1920. "Pier Tax Refunder Saves City Thousands," *Hudson Observer*, March 12, 1924, found in *World War I Scrapbook*, Hoboken Public Library.

266. Hoboken finally gained control of the piers in 1952 and immediately leased the facilities to the Port Authority of New York for one dollar per year for fifty years. "U.S. Plans to Lease 6 Piers to Hoboken; City Wins Fight for Control of Docks Seized in 1917 From German Concerns," *New York Times*, May 1, 1952, 59; "2 Leasings Speed Hoboken Pier Use; Old German Center Seized by U.S. Is Turned Over by City to the Port Authority," *New York Times*, September 25, 1952, 53.

267. "To Grant Relief to the City of Hoboken." Also see "Confident That Piers Bill Drawn By Fallon Has Better Chance Than Predecessors," *New Jersey Observer*, April 28, 1924, found in *World War I Scrapbook*, Hoboken Public Library. Hoboken initially attempted to lease the piers from the federal government with the idea of then renting the facilities to a private shipping company, receiving some revenue in the form of rent, but this idea went nowhere.

268. Doig, *Empire on the Hudson*, 199.

269. "Leviathan Singed, Army Piers Burned, Soldier Dead Saved, New York and Jersey Firemen Battle with Flames Lighting the Hudson a Mile," *New York Times*, August 25, 1921, 1; "Hoboken Fire Laid to Short Circuit, This Is Most Probable Cause Found, but Army Board Continues Investigation," *New York Times*, August 26, 1921, 2. After the 1900 pier fire, the North German Lloyd company immediately rebuilt its piers and made them fireproof, which saved those piers in 1921.

270. Thirteenth U.S. Census, *Population Reports by States*, 151; Fourteenth U.S. Census, *Population*, 652–53.

271. Fourteenth U.S. Census, *Population*, 652–53.

272. Ibid., 657.

273. Jersey City, *Hoboken Directory*, 1251–1252.

274. The Schnackenbergs immigrated from Bremen, Germany, separately in the mid-1920s and bought their restaurant at a bankruptcy sale

during the Great Depression. "Schnackenberg's Luncheonette, Never a Plain Coke, Recollections of Betty Silvani," *Hoboken Chapbook* (Hoboken Historical Museum, 2001), 3.

275. In 1920, Hoboken had 44,418 native-born whites, while only 37,593 in 1930 (the decline for foreign-born whites between 1920 and 1930 was only 730 persons). Fifteenth U.S. Census, *Reports by States*, 207, 210. Note that in the census of 1930, pp. 208–209 of Table 18 are missing, and Table 19 only lists select countries and does not include Germany or Ireland.

276. Fisher, *On the Irish Waterfront*.

277. Ibid., 32, quoting Bob Leach, *The Frank Hague Picture Book* (Jersey City: Jersey City Historical Project, 1998), vii.

278. Fisher, *On the Irish Waterfront*, 31, about Jersey City "Boss" Frank Hague, quoting William Lemmey, "Bossism in Jersey City: The Kenny Years, 1949–1972" (PhD diss., City University of New York, 1972), 48.

279. Fisher, *On the Irish Waterfront*, 38–39.

280. R.L. Polk & Co. City Directory, *Classified Business Directory*, 1925–1926, 1427.

281. *A Nice Tavern*, 19.

282. "The Progressives vs. The Political Machine in Hoboken," in Foster and Clark, *Hoboken*, 72; "Ex-Mayor M'Feely of Hoboken, Was 68," *New York Times*, August 10, 1949, 10.

283. "The Progressives vs. The Political Machine in Hoboken," in Foster and Clark, *Hoboken*, 73.

284. Sixteenth U.S. Census, *Characteristics of the Population*, 30–79.

285. Fisher, *On the Irish Waterfront*, 145. Varacalli, "Ethnic Politics in Jersey City," 1983, also notes Hague's preference for Irish Americans over Italians.

286. Fisher, *On the Irish Waterfront*, 19. As Fisher notes, most longshoremen working in the Port of New York and New Jersey were Catholic and often Irish. Burrows and Wallace, *Gotham*, 1123, note that as early as the late 1880s, New York waterfront bosses began hiring Italians, often during strikes, to try to break the Irish lock on longshore jobs. Technically, a longshoreman worked on the dock itself, while a stevedore worked in the cargo hold of the ship; before containerization, longshoremen and stevedores were represented by different unions.

287. Fisher, *On the Irish Waterfront*, 18–21. Corruption became part of the shapeup because would-be dockworkers often had to pay bribes to foremen to get hired and also frequently had to borrow money from loan sharks

in order to afford the necessary bribes. By the 1950s, the International Longshoremen's Association (ILA) more resembled a criminal syndicate than a labor organization.

288. Fisher, *On the Irish Waterfront*, 26–27.

289. Fifteenth U.S. Census, *Characteristics of the Population*, 199. Although these figures include all adult aliens in Hoboken, the fact that a large number of foreign-born residents were Italian suggests that most Italians in Hoboken were slow to naturalize, as Italians were elsewhere in the United States.

290. Sixteenth U.S. Census, *Characteristics of the Population*, 876.

291. Warren Grover, *Nazis in Newark*.

292. "Time Marches...Backward!" *New York Times*, September 2, 2010, www.nytimes.com/2010/09/03/movies/03newsreel.html?_r=1&scp=1&sq=nazi%20films%20hoboken&st=cse (accessed November 14, 2010).

293. Hoboken's post-McFeely mayors have been (as of 2011): Louis De Pascale in 1965 (election set aside by a judge); Silvio Failla for two months in 1965; Louis De Pascale again from 1965 to 1973; Steve Cappiello from 1973 to 1985; Thomas Vezzetti from 1985 to 1988; Patrick Pasculli from 1988 to 1993; Anthony Russo from 1993 to 2001; David Roberts from 2001 to 2010; Peter Cammarano for July 2010 (until his arrest and resignation); and Dawn Zimmer (as of August 2010).

CHAPTER 8

294. Korrol, *Colonia to Community*, 36.

295. Ibid., 46.

296. Wyman, *Round-Trip to America*, 10, 82–83.

297. Olivieri interview. Puerto Rico's property tax, which is low due to failure to reassess over many years, also encourages this.

298. Michael Lapp, "Migration Division of Puerto Rico," 199. Although the first Puerto Ricans migrated to the mainland in the 1920s, most Spanish-speaking immigrants arrived in the New York area in the 1950s. There were few visible reminders of the cultural institutions that earlier Spanish-speaking immigrants had created, such as the Masonic lodge *Amparo Latino* (Latin Relief), established in 1919, or the club *Faro de las Antillas* (Lighthouse of the Antilles) founded in 1928, according to Duany, *Puerto Rican Nation*.

299. Shaw, *Immigration and Ethnicity*, 59.

300. "Total Number of Immigrants by Year, 1820–2007," http://teacher.scholastic.com/activities/immigration/pdfs/1820-2007stats.pdf (accessed August 10, 2010).

301. Doig, *Empire on the Hudson*, 374–76. Containerization dramatically reduced the number of dockworkers because goods were never unloaded from trucks or rail cars and then reloaded onto the ship; rather, the entire truck trailers were lifted onto specially designed ships by crane. Hoboken's piers also did not have the space to accommodate the equipment needed for container shipping.

302. "An Interpretation of Hoboken's Population Trends," in Foster and Clark, *Hoboken*, 55–56.

303. "The Great Migration," in Dolan and Vidal, *Puerto Rican and Cuban Catholics*, 57–58.

304. "An Interpretation of Hoboken's Population Trends," in Foster and Clark, *Hoboken*, 54; Bierbaum, "Hoboken, a Come-Back City," 55.

305. "An Interpretation of Hoboken's Population Trends," in Foster and Clark, *Hoboken*, 56; Eighteenth U.S. Census, *Characteristics of the Population*, 32–277, 284. Note that in 1960, the census stated that Hoboken had 848 residents from "other America," which could include Puerto Rico.

306. Nineteenth U.S. Census, *Characteristics of the Population*. The census by this point distinguished between "persons of Spanish language," "other persons of Spanish surname," "persons of Spanish mother tongue" and "persons of Puerto Rican birth or parentage."

307. *Jersey Journal*, May 30, 1972, 27.

308. See for example Padilla interview.

309. Guzman interview.

310. Shirak, *Our Way*, 56, 117; Olivieri interview.

311. Guglielmolli interview.

312. Centennial of St. Joseph's Parish.

313. "The Great Migration," in Dolan and Vidal, *Puerto Rican and Cuban Catholics*, 73.

314. "The Attempt to Americanize Puerto Rico and the Problem of Identity," in Dolan and Vidal, *Puerto Rican and Cuban Catholics*, 32–33.

315. Ibid., 37.

316. "The Great Migration," in Dolan and Vidal, *Puerto Rican and Cuban Catholics*, 62.

317. Vecoli, *People of New Jersey*, 220–30.

318. Immigration Chart, Eighteenth U.S. Census, *General Population Characteristics*, 32–93.

319. Olivieri interview.

320. Sixteenth U.S. Census, *Characteristics of the Population*, 876; Eighteenth U.S. Census, *General Population Characteristics*, 32–93.

321. Light-skinned Puerto Ricans sometimes found themselves able to pass as Italian. Rivera and Olivieri interview; Guzman interview; Forman interview; Padilla interview.

322. Forman interview.

323. Jacobson, *Delivered Vacant*.

324. Forman interview.

325. "The Gospel According to Gentrification," *Jersey Journal*, April 2, 1988, 17.

326. Morales interview; Keim interview. Applied was an early participant in the federal Section 8 program, but paid off its forty-year mortgage from the federal Housing and Urban Development Department in 1998, allowing it to charge market rates for many of its more than twenty-five hundred units in Hoboken. Applied continues, however, to provide low- and middle-income housing through agreements it has with the New Jersey Department of Community Affairs and HUD. "Looking into Applied Lawsuit. Affordable Housing Case Could Be Decided This Week," *Hudson Reporter*, March 10, 2001.

BIBLIOGRAPHY

Albion, Robert Greenhalgh. *The Rise of New York Port, 1815–1860*. New York: Charles Scribner's Sons, 1939.

Aleinikoff, Thomas Alexander, David A. Martin and Hiroshi Motomura. *Immigration and Citizenship: Process and Policy*. 5th ed. St. Paul, MN: Thomson West, 2003.

Annual Report of the Commissioners of Emigration of the State of New York, for the Year Ending December 31, 1855. New York: William C. Bryant & Co., printers, 1856.

Beck, Henry Charlton. *Tales and Towns of Northern New Jersey*. New Brunswick, NJ: Rutgers University Press, 1983.

Bierbaum, Martin A. "Hoboken, a Come-Back City: A Study of Urban Revitalization in the 1970s." PhD diss., Rutgers University, State University of New Jersey, 1980.

Burrows, Edwin G., and Mike Wallace. *Gotham: A History of New York City to 1898*. New York: Oxford University Press, 1999. See esp. chap. 42, "City of Immigrants."

Cahalan, Brigid A. "Hoboken: A City in Transition: An Annotated Selective Listing of Source Materials: 1855–1983." Research paper, Queens College, CUNY, 1983.

Cavaioli, Frank J., Salvatore J. Lagumina, Salvatore Primeggia and Joseph A. Varacalli, eds. *The Italian American Experience: An Encyclopedia*. New York: Garland Press, 2000.

Centennial of St. Joseph's Parish, 1871–1971, October 24, 1971. Folder 7; "Hoboken-St. Joseph's Parish," Box 52, Parish Files; "Hoboken-St. Francis of Assisi, Hoboken-St. Joseph's Parish, Hoboken-SS. Peter & Paul," Record Group 10.5. Seton Hall University Archives and Special Collections Center, South Orange, New Jersey.

Coffman, Edward M. *The War to End All Wars: The American Military Experience in World War I.* Oxford, UK: Oxford University Press, 1968.

Cohn, Raymond L. *Mass Migration Under Sail, European Immigration to the Antebellum United States.* Cambridge, UK: Cambridge University Press, 2009.

Cudahy, Brian J. *Over and Back: The History of Ferryboats in New York Harbor.* New York: Fordham University Press, 1990.

Daniels, Roger. *Guarding the Golden Door: American Immigration Policy and Immigrants Since 1882.* New York: Hill and Wang, 2004.

Doig, Jameson W. *Empire on the Hudson: Entrepreneurial Vision and Political Power at the Port of New York Authority.* New York: Columbia University Press, 2001.

Dolan, Jay, and Jaime R. Vidal, eds. *Puerto Rican and Cuban Catholics in the U.S., 1900–1965.* Notre Dame, IN: University of Notre Dame Press, 1994.

Duany, Jorge. *The Puerto Rican Nation on the Move: Identities on the Island and in the United States.* Chapel Hill: University of North Carolina Press, 2002.

Eighteenth U.S. Census. *General Population Characteristics, New Jersey, Table 21—Characteristics of the Population, for Standard Metropolitan Statistical Areas, Urbanized Areas, and Urban Places and Selected Townships of 10,000 or More: 1960, Hoboken.* Washington, D.C.: Government Printing Office, 1960.

Eleventh U.S. Census. *Part 1, General Tables, Cities, Towns, Villages, and Boroughs, Table 7, Increase in Population of Cities Having 25,000 or More in 1890, at Each Census, 1790–1890, Hoboken.* Washington, D.C.: Government Printing Office, 1890.

Espenshade, Thomas J. *A Stone's Throw from Ellis Island: Economic Implications of Immigration to New Jersey.* Lanham, MD: University Press of America, 1994.

Fifteenth U.S. Census. *Characteristics of the Population, Part 2, Section 3, New Jersey, Composition and Characteristics, Table 15—Composition of the Population, for Urban Places of 10,000 or more: 1930–Continued.* Washington, D.C.: Government Printing Office, 1930.

Fisher, James T. *On the Irish Waterfront: The Crusader, the Movie, and the Soul of the Port of New York.* Ithaca, NY: Cornell University Press, 2009.

Flagg, Thomas R. "From Farm and Marsh to Cityscape: The Railroads Transformed Hudson County." Paper presented at the Come Home to History Hudson County History Fair, Jersey City, New Jersey, October 9, 2010.

———. *New York Harbor Railroads in Color*. 2 vols. Scotch Plains, NJ: Morning Sun Books, 2000, 2002). Available online at www.trainweb.org/rmig/litera.html.

Flynn, Joseph M. *The Catholic Church in New Jersey*. Morristown, NJ, 1904.

Foster, Edward Halsey, and Geoffrey W. Clark, eds. *Hoboken: A Collection of Essays*. New York: Irvington Publishers, 1975. See esp. "An Interpretation of Hoboken's Population Trends, 1856–1970" and "The Progressives vs. The Political Machine in Hoboken, 1911–1915."

Furer, Howard B. "'Heaven, Hell or Hoboken': The Effects of World War I on a New Jersey City." *New Jersey History* 92, no. 3 (Autumn 1974): 147–69.

Garis, Roy L. *Immigration Restriction: A Study of the Opposition to and Regulation of Immigration into the United States*. New York: Macmillan Company, 1927.

Govorchin, Gerald Gilbert, ed. *Americans from Yugoslavia*. Gainesville: University Press of Florida, 1961.

Grover, Warren. *Nazis in Newark*. Piscataway, NJ: Transaction Publishers, 2003.

Halo Over Hoboken: The Memoirs of John Perkins Field as told to John Leroy Bailey. New York: Exposition Press, 1955.

Heaney, John J. *The Bicentennial Comes to Hoboken*. N.p., 1976. Call letters N974.928H 1976.

Henry, Sharon. "Germans, Irish, Italians, Puerto Ricans, and Then... Waves of Immigration Have Shaped Hoboken Board of Trade. *History of Hoboken*. Hoboken, NJ: Inquirer Printers, 1907.

"Hoboken's History." *Hudson Reporter*, March 28, 2005.

Howe, Frederic C. *The Confessions of a Reformer*. Kent, OH: Kent State University Press, 1988.

Immigration Chart. http://teacher.scholastic.com/activities/immigration/pdfs/1820-2007stats.pdf.

Jacobson, Nora. *Delivered Vacant*. Film, 1992.

Jersey City, Hoboken Directory, 1915, Part 5, Classified Businesses; Polk's City Directory, Jersey City and Hoboken, 1925–1926, Classified Business Directory; "Saloons, Hoboken," R.L. Polk & Co. (1925–26), Classified Business Directory. New Jersey Room of the Jersey City Main Library, Jersey City, New Jersey.

Johnson, Malcolm. *On the Waterfront*. New York: Chamberlain Brothers, Penguin Group, 2005.

Kapp, Friedrich. *Immigration and the Commissioners of Emigration*. New York: Arno Press and the New York Times, 1969.

Kennedy, David M. *Over Here: The First World War and American Society*. Oxford, UK: Oxford University Press, 1980.

Korrol, Virginia E. Sánchez. *From Colonia to Community: The History of Puerto Ricans in New York City, 1917–1948*. Westport, CT: Greenwood Press, 1983.

Kraut, Allan. *Silent Travelers: Germs, Genes, and the "Immigrant Menace."* Baltimore, MD: Johns Hopkins University Press, 1994.

Lapp, Michael. "The Migration Division of Puerto Rico and Puerto Ricans in New York City, 1948–1969." In *Immigration to New York*, edited by William Pencak, Selma Berrol and Randall M. Miller. Philadelphia: Balch Institute Press, 1991.

Luebke, Frederick C. *Bonds of Loyalty: German-Americans and World War I*. Dekalb: Northern Illinois University Press, 1974.

Massachusetts Department of Education. *Annual Report of the Division of Immigration and Americanization for the Year ending November 30, 1921*. Boston: Wright & Potter Printing Co., 1922.

Miller, Randall M., ed. *Germans in America*. Philadelphia: German Society of Pennsylvania, 1984.

Millman, Chad. *The Detonators: The Secret Plot to Destroy America and an Epic Hunt for Justice*. New York: Little, Brown & Co., 2008.

Moltmann, Günter, ed. *Germans to America: 300 Years of Immigration, 1683–1983*. Stuttgart, Germany: Institut fur Auslandsbeziehungen, 1982.

Nadel, Stanley. *Little Germany, Ethnicity, Religion and Class in New York City, 1845–80*. Urbana: University of Illinois Press, 1990.

Nelson, Michael. "Ol' Red, White, and Blue Eyes: Frank Sinatra and the American Presidency." *Popular Music and Society* 24 (2000).

The New "Red Book" Information and Trolley Guide to Jersey City, Hoboken, Bayonne, West Hoboken, Union Hill, West New York, Weehawken, Guttenberg, North Bergen, Secaucus. With indexed map. New York: Interstate Map Co., 1922.

New York–New Jersey Committee of the North American Civic League for Immigrants. December 1909–March 1911; December 1, 1909–February 1913. New York, n.d.

New York State Department of Labor. *Bureau of Industries and Immigration, First Annual Report 1910–1911*. Albany: New York State Department of Labor, 1912).

New York Times

A Nice Tavern: Remembering the Continental Hotel and the Union Club, Recollections of Paul Samperi. Chapbook. Hoboken, NJ: Hoboken Historical Museum, 2008.

Nineteenth U.S. Census. *Characteristics of the Population, New Jersey, Table P-2—Social Characteristics of the Population, Census Tracts, Nativity, Parentage, & Country of Origin*. Washington, D.C.: Government Printing Office, 1970.

Ninth U.S. Census. *The General Tables of Aggregate Population, Table 3: Population 1870–1850, in Each State and Territory, by Civil Divisions Less than Counties, as White and Colored (1870–1850), and Native and Foreign (1850)—New Jersey, Hoboken*. Washington, D.C.: Government Printing Office, 1870.

Procter, Mary, and Bill Matuszeski. *Gritty Cities: A Second Look at Allentown, Bethlehem, Bridgeport, Hoboken, Lancaster, Norwich, Paterson, Reading, Trenton, Troy, Waterbury, Wilmington*. Philadelphia: Temple University Press, 1978.

Pupin, Michael. *From Immigrant to Inventor*. New York: Charles Scribner's Sons, 1923.

Quinn, Dermot. *The Irish in New Jersey, Four Centuries of American Life*. New Brunswick, NJ: Rutgers University Press, 2004.

Report of the Commissioners of Emigration of the State of New York, Made to the Legislature January 23, 1850. New York: Casper C. Childs, printer, 1850.

Report of the Commission of Immigration of the State of New Jersey, Appointed Pursuant to the Provisions of Chapter 362 of the Laws of 1911. Trenton, NJ: MacGrellish & Quigley, state printers, 1914.

Revised Laws Concerning Passengers in Vessels Coming to the City of New York and for the Protection of Emigrants, Condensed and Revised by Order of the Commission of Emigration. New York: Casper C. Childs, printer, 1850.

Sanborn Map Company. *Insurance Maps of Hudson County, New Jersey*. Vol. 7. New York: Sanborn Map Co., 1906–1961.

"Schnackenberg's Luncheonette, Never a Plain Coke, Recollections of Betty Silvani." *Hoboken Chapbook*. Hoboken, NJ: Hoboken Historical Museum, 2001.

Shaw, Douglas V. *Immigration and Ethnicity in New Jersey History*. Trenton: New Jersey Historical Commission, 1994.

Shaw, William H. *History of Essex and Hudson Counties, New Jersey*. Vol. 2, *Charles B. Brush, City of Hoboken*. Philadelphia: Everts & Peck, 1884.

Shirak, Ed, Jr. *Our Way: In Honor of Frank Sinatra*. Hoboken, NJ: Lepores Publishing, 1995.

Sixteenth U.S. Census. *Characteristics of the Population, Part 4, Minnesota–New Mexico: New Jersey, Table 31, Composition of the Population, for Urban Places of 10,000 to 100,000: 1940*. Washington, D.C: Government Printing Office, 1940.

Sixth U.S. Census. *Compendium of the Enumeration of the Inhabitants and Statistics of the United States, New Jersey, Recapitulation of the Aggregate Amount of Each Description of Persons within the District of New Jersey, by Counties and Principal Towns*. Washington, D.C.: Government Printing Office, 1840.

Smith, Harrell Hevernor, and H. Guy Herring. *The Bureau of Immigration, Its History, Activities, and Organization, for the Institute for Government Research*. Service Monographs of the United States Government, No. 30. Baltimore, MD: Johns Hopkins Press, 1924.

Sobel, Robert, and John Raimo, eds. *Biographical Directory of the Governors of the United States, 1789–1978*. Vol. 3, s.v. "Leon Abbett." Westport, CT: Meckler Books, 1978.

Steiner, Edward A. *On the Trail of the Immigrant*. New York: Fleming H. Revell, 1906.

Tenth U.S. Census. *General Population Tables, Population, by Race, Sex, and Nativity, Table IX, Population, as Native and Foreign, of Cities and Towns of 4,000 Inhabitants and Upwards: 1880–1870, Hoboken*. Washington, D.C., Government Printing Office, 1880.

———. *Report on the Social Statistics of Cities, Part I: The New England and Middle Atlantic States, Part II: The Middle States, New Jersey, Hoboken-Trenton*. Washington, D.C.: Government Printing Office, 1886.

Thernstrom, Stephan, ed. *Harvard Encyclopedia of American Ethnic Groups*. Cambridge, MA: Belknap Press of Harvard University Press, 1980.

Thirteenth U.S. Census. *Population: Reports by States Nebraska-Wyoming, Section 1, Reports by States with Statistics for Counties, Cities, & Other Civil Divisions: New Jersey, Table V—Composition and Characteristics of the Population for Wards of Cities of 50,000 or More—Continued, Hoboken*. Washington, D.C.: Government Printing Office, 1910.

Tichenor, Daniel J. *Dividing Lines: The Politics of Immigration Control in America*. Princeton, NJ: Princeton University Press, 2002.

Trommler, Frank, and Joseph McVeigh, eds. *Americans and the Germans: An Assessment of a Three-Hundred-Year History*. Vol. 1, *Immigration, Language, Ethnicity*. Philadelphia: University of Pennsylvania, 1985.

United States Bureau of the Census. www.census.gov/prod/www/abs/decennial.

United States Citizenship and Immigration Services. U.S. Department of Homeland Security website. http://uscis.gov/graphics/aboutus/history/ April 1912.

Van Winkle, Daniel. *History of Municipalities of Hudson County, 1630–1923*. Vol. 1, *Historical-Biographical*. Chicago: Lewis Historical Publishing Co., 1924.

Varacalli, Joseph A. "Ethnic Politics in Jersey City: The Changing Nature of Irish-Italian Relations, 1917–1983." Paper presented at the 16th Annual Conference of the American Italian Historical Association, State University of Albany, November 11–12, 1983.

Vecoli, Rudolph J. *The People of New Jersey*. Princeton, NJ: D. Van Nostrand Co., 1965.

West, Herbert Faulkner, ed. *The Autobiography of Robert Watchorn*. Oklahoma City, OK: Robert Watchorn Charities, Ltd., 1928.

Winfield, Charles H. *History of the County of Hudson, New Jersey, From Its Earliest Settlement to the Present Time*. New York: Kennard and Hay Stationary Manufacturing and Printing Co., 1874.

———. *Hopoghan Hackingh: Hoboken, a Pleasure Resort for Old New York*. New York: Caxton Press, 1895.

Witcover, Jules. *Sabotage at Black Tom: Imperial Germany's Secret War in America, 1914–1917*. Chapel Hill, NC: Algonquin Books of Chapel Hill, 1989.

Wittke, Carl. *Refugees of Revolution: The German Forty-Eighters in America*. Philadelphia: University of Pennsylvania Press, 1952.

Wyman, Mark. *Round-Trip to America: The Immigrants Return to Europe, 1880–1930*. Ithaca, NY: Cornell University Press, 1993.

Zolberg, Aristide R. *A Nation by Design: Immigration Policy in the Fashioning of America*. Cambridge, MA: Harvard University Press, 2006.

ORAL HISTORY INTERVIEWS

All interviews were conducted by the author and are archived at the Hoboken Historical Museum and Center for Puerto Rican Studies, Hunter College (CUNY).

Ballester, Ivonne, December 28, 2009.

Crespo, Delia, December 1, 2009.

Forman, Jerry and Elizabeth, December 14, 2009.

Guglielmolli, Father Mike, February 19, 2010.

Guzman, George and Carmen, December 11, 2009.

Hunnewinkel, Sister Norberta, February 2, 2010.

Keim, Ines Garcia, December 16, 2009.

Morales, Raul, January 8, 2010.

Padilla, Angel and Gloria, January 26, 2010.

Rivera, Socorro, and Teofilo "Tom" Olivieri, November 23, 2009.

About the Author

Christina A. Ziegler-McPherson is a public historian in the New York City area. She holds a PhD in history from the University of California, Santa Barbara, is the author of *Americanization in the States: Immigrant Social Welfare Policy, Citizenship, and National Identity in the United States, 1908–1929* (University Press of Florida, 2009) and has published several encyclopedia essays about immigration. She has done historical research for such institutions as the Hoboken Historical Museum and the Museum of the City of New York and has taught history at Empire State College (SUNY).

Visit us at
www.historypress.net